*The Little Manual
of Perfect Prayer
and Adoration*

Fr. Joseph-Marie Perrin, O.P.

The Little Manual of Perfect Prayer and Adoration

SOPHIA INSTITUTE PRESS®

Manchester, New Hampshire

The Little Manual of Perfect Prayer and Adoration is an abridged edition of *Living with God* (St. Louis, Missouri: B. Herder Book Company, 1961). This 2002 edition by Sophia Institute Press® does not include the section entitled "Preliminaries" from the 1961 edition and contains minor editorial revisions to the text.

Copyright © 1961 Aquin Press;
2002 Dominican Province of Toulouse

Printed in the United States of America

Cover design by Lorraine Bilodeau

Sophia Institute Press®
Box 5284, Manchester, NH 03108
1-800-888-9344
www.sophiainstitute.com

Nihil obstat: Daniel Diuvesteijn, S.T.D., *Censor deputatus*
Imprimatur: E. Morrogh Bernard, L.C.L., *Vic. Gen.*
Westminster, June 2, 1958

Library of Congress Cataloging-in-Publication Data

Perrin, Joseph Marie, 1905-
   [Vivre avec Dieu. English]
   The little manual of perfect prayer and adoration /
      Joseph-Marie Perrin.
         p. cm.
   Abridged ed. of: Living with God. 1961.
   Includes bibliographical references.
   ISBN 1-928832-58-X
   1. Prayer. I. Title.
   BV210.3 .P4713 2002
   248.3′2 — dc21   2002004310

02 03 04 05 06 07 08 09 10 9 8 7 6 5 4 3 2 1

❧

Contents

❧

Part One: The elements of prayer

⊱

Part Two: The life of prayer

⊱

Part Three: Achieving life with God

⊱

✴

Preface

The essence of Christian life is the new relationship with God created by a man's union with Christ. When he becomes a member of the Mystical Body, he embarks upon a new life that "looks toward God."[1] He has eternal life, and he knows it. He sets about living with this knowledge, and he is established in truth and joy.

Prayer is nothing other than this relationship with God, conscious and lived. Rodin was quite right when

---

[1] Cf. Rom. 6:10. The biblical quotations in the following pages are taken from the Douay-Rheims edition of the Old and New Testaments. Where applicable, quotations have been cross-referenced with the differing names and enumeration in the Revised Standard Version, using the following symbol: (RSV =).

he imagined the Christian molded by prayer. Just as he is born of water and of the Spirit,[2] so he lives by prayer.

Nothing would be more foreign to the spirit of Christianity than to think of prayer as a restricted exercise, a technique, or a practice. From Christ we have learned "that we ought always to pray and not to faint."[3]

Did not His final words, together with His last look on earth, consist of the promise "I am with you all days"?[4] A Christian knows that His "with you" means with the whole of His Church (for the Apostles were there on the mount of the Ascension with the disciples and the holy women) and also with every one of those who, through the course of the centuries, were to believe in Him through the Apostles' words. Each of them discovers that the name of Christ to which he clings means, in God's language "Emmanuel, which being interpreted is God with us."[5]

Does not the whole of our earthly life lean toward the meeting with God? "For the Lord Himself shall

[2] Cf. John 3:5.
[3] Luke 18:1.
[4] Matt. 28:20.
[5] Matt. 1:23.

come down from Heaven with commandment and with the voice of an archangel and with the trumpet of God; and the dead who are in Christ shall rise first. Then we who are alive, who are left, shall be taken up together with them in the clouds to meet Christ, into the air, and so shall we be always with the Lord."[6]

In the light of St. Paul's description, we can understand the fine remark of one of the first Christian authors: "As to the times for prayer, nothing has been laid down except that we must pray at all times and in all places."[7] This injunction leads to no depreciation of prayer; the fact of its being carried on continually does not make it commonplace; rather, it makes life divine by establishing it in God.

Prayer is a great and a precious thing, since the Father looks for it; it is something superhuman, since only in spirit can we be united with Him who is Spirit. The impossibility of our conversing with a man whose language we do not know; the difficulty of talking in any but a superficial way to someone whose thoughts and

---

[6] 1 Thess. 4:15-16.

[7] Tertullian (c. 155-c. 225; Christian apologist and writer), Ml. l. 1192 A.

feelings we do not know, the misunderstandings arising from interviews such as these ought to make us alive to the mystery of prayer and to the awe of this conversation with God. "We know not what we should pray for as we ought; but the Spirit Himself asketh for us with unspeakable groanings."[8] We must adore "in spirit and in truth."[9] "The conversation God likes is the silence of love," said St. John of the Cross.[10]

⚜

Let your prayer
embrace the whole world

Further, although this relationship with God is personal, it nevertheless concerns the whole world. It concerns it first of all in that, far from being mutually exclusive, the terms *personal* and *communal* are strict correlatives. Only a peculiarly erroneous view could suppose that the deepening of individual personality could impoverish the community. On the contrary, as a

---

[8] Rom. 8:26.

[9] John 4:23.

[10] St. John of the Cross (1542-1591), mystical doctor and founder of the Discalced Carmelites.

human being becomes more deeply personal, he is able to communicate himself more liberally. This elementary truth, proved in the human sphere, is even more valid for the new personality forged by the fire of the Spirit into a living relationship with the most personal of all Persons, with God, who is in His unity Father, Son, and Holy Spirit.

This is not all; prayer is one of the Christian's duties; by prayer, he discharges the formidable responsibility of having been invested in Christ with a "royal priesthood";[11] if he fails, some of his brethren's aspirations will be unable to reach God, and some favors on their behalf will remain unasked. The Gospel cannot be heard if there is no preacher, but preachers are wanting when there is no one to voice God's words anew.[12] It was already declared in the Old Testament that a people lacking the activity of the prophets was given over to folly.[13] As the words of the Lord's Prayer itself show us, God has entrusted His own interests to us by linking our prayer with His most fundamental purposes.

[11] Cf. 1 Pet. 2:9.
[12] Cf. 1 Pet. 4:11.
[13] Cf. Prov. 29:18.

To those who are surprised at this, Fr. Sertillanges answers, "If the principle of the arrangement of things is God and if God is love, then prayer addressed to love can, together with Him, dispose of all things, determine what is to happen, fulfill desires, not in time, where the plans of Providence are carried out, but in eternity, where they are designed."[14]

These truths are essential, and they belong to all time. A Christian is one who is with God, who treasures in his heart the words of farewell that Christ pronounced to His people, lifting His hands to bless them at the moment when He entered into His glory: "And behold, I am with you all days, even to the consummation of the world."[15]

⚜

Lead others to God by living in Him

Yet it is clear that these truths contain something even more striking when set beside the tremendous effort made by militant atheism to drive God from the world. Many declare themselves to be "without God,"

---

[14] Fr. A. G. Sertillanges, *La Vie Interieure*.

[15] Matt. 28:20.

taking for their motto and program what is the ultimate wretchedness and the very definition of Hell. The Christian has "eternal life,"[16] as we have said, and he knows it; he must, in return, wish to live more intensely his life with God, knowing that this is also the best service he can give his brethren by making them share his joy and his life. Movement cannot be better expressed than by walking; God can never be better demonstrated than by our living in Him. Fire reveals itself by burning; energy from above by lifting; God, by making the life of His people godlike.

Present-day circumstances should make all Christians feel the duty of being with God so that they "may declare" to the world "His virtues, who hath called you out of darkness into His marvelous light."[17] It would even seem that those living fully in the world have the best opportunity for giving this testimony. No one can excuse himself from it on the grounds that it is impossible.

Faced with such demands, some people refuse, preferring to pile their responsibilities on a select few, forgetting to ask themselves who makes up this select few

[16] 1 John 5:11.
[17] 1 Pet. 2:9.

when it comes to the kingdom of God; forgetting that all baptized people are included in this "holy generation . . . this holy nation."[18] In order to discredit forever the empty excuses that poison so many of His people, Christ chose a Samaritan woman, publicly dishonored by the fact of her having had five husbands, who was busy getting water for her household; to her He entrusted the loftiest revelation about the new prayer that was going to be born into the world — namely, the adoration in spirit and in truth.

Prayer free from garrulity and said in the sight of the Father, who sees what is secret, is expounded in the Sermon on the Mount, together with most of the other teaching on prayer — although some of it was kept for the confidence of the disciples, and it was for their joy and in their presence that the prayer after the Last Supper was said.

✤

Let prayer transform your life
I shall be content if I can help some of those who are struggling with difficulties, and who have not responded

18 1 Pet. 2:9.

to the call, to understand that prayer is not a labor that will overburden their already heavily committed lives, but a spirit that will transfigure life and give it vitality and beauty; that it is not a complicated technique like algebra, but a personal discovery very near to everyone.

The science of prayer does not answer "What am I to do?" but the question "Master, where dwellest Thou?"[19] Where can we find You and learn to know You intimately? It is a question and a quest of love.

That first meeting, the first exchange of conversation between Christ and His disciples, gives us the meaning of prayer: "Master, where dwellest Thou?" This is the question that is answered throughout the Gospel that was written by the man who asked the question. "That you also may have fellowship with us and our fellowship may be with the Father and with His Son, Jesus Christ."[20]

Or again, the desire comes upon us as it did upon the disciples when they saw their Master returning from His prayer: "Teach us to pray."[21] But it is a small thing to base our prayer on human aspirations; it ought to be

[19] John 1:38.
[20] 1 John 1:3.
[21] Luke 11:1.

based on the divine ideal and to correspond to its designs. It is impossible to give God anything except by receiving from Him. "To receive from God," Bossuet[22] explains in one of his letters, "is to give to Him, and, since He has no need of benefits from us, all He asks of us is to receive those that He gives us."

The words of the Gospel itself, about those who dwell in God, about the establishing of God in us, about the continuousness of prayer, rule out any concepts that would reduce life with God to a restricted exercise; and they have formed the subject most often expounded by Christian authors, few of whom have not written about prayer and about the Lord's Prayer. It follows that in embarking on this theme, we are certain of treading a path already clearly marked out. We know that there is nothing new to be said; we know that we cannot rise adequately to the subject; we know that we cannot even repeat all that has been said before. But it was felt that private notes that had helped a few Christians living in the midst of this world of tumult to make their life a life of prayer could be helpful to others; and from this, this book was born.

[22] Jacques Benigne Bossuet (1627-1724), Bishop of Meaux.

Preface

The essential thought expressed in these pages is that love alone — the love of God and of our neighbor for God's sake, two loves that are really one — makes us exist in God, and that all human life, even the most burdensome and the most depressing, can become love. I would like, together with others of my own generation, to become one of those people who meditate on this life with God that has been offered to them by Christ as the secret to joy and happiness.

The plan of this work is very simple: the preliminary chapters set the problem by considering God's plan of uniting us to Himself, together with the Christian's position in the world of today. The first part studies the directives given by the Gospel for all prayer; the second seeks to show how the whole of life can be and should be with God. The third part examines some special methods of achieving this.

God is with us. May He grant us to be with Him.

Christmas 1956

❧

The Little Manual
of Perfect Prayer
and Adoration

Part One

❦

The elements
of prayer

Chapter One

ৡ

Understand your relationship with God

Prayer is a "conversation with God." Hence, it is impossible to understand Christian prayer, to glimpse its truth, its beauty, and the demands it makes without knowing what kind of relationship unites God to man. It is from the infinite freshness of this relationship that prayer takes its proper nature. Except in this light, it can be neither explained nor practiced. St. Francis de Sales's[23] now classic saying — which is all the more worthy of attention because this saint's mission was to open a school of holiness in the Church — throws light on this reflection: "Prayer is an affair of love." St. Teresa sees in

[23] St. Francis de Sales (1567-1622), Bishop of Geneva.

prayer "that look where their love is read"[24] between God who loves and the loving soul.

There is nothing original in these phrases, for they state, in one way or another, what all the Church's spiritual writers have declared, but the deeper meanings of such formulas can be grasped only by someone who knows the infinite freshness of the spirit-created love with which a Christian loves God.

Prayer's dimensions are determined by three points: we are loved by God; we love Him; and we desire to love Him.

❧

Respond to God's love for you

First of all, there is this infinite love of which we are conscious, and which invites us to approach Him in love and in union with all that He loves. The relations with God and the resulting dialogue come not from man's initiative, but from God's free gift. If we approach God, it is not that we have traveled leagues in search of Him, wearing out our feet on the dusty paths, or have

---

[24] St. Teresa of Avila (1515-1582; Carmelite mystic), *Life*, ch. 27.

eaten out our hearts on the wings of desire. He was there, on the threshold all the time; before we opened our eyes, He was watching and waiting for us; before we called Him, He was there. It is He who seeks out His adorers.

The position we are in with regard to God is the position that He Himself placed us in. Whatever form his prayer may take, the Christian prays because he is beloved, and no prayer that has its origins elsewhere can be a true prayer. Therefore, the disciple will pray through love.

To pray through love is to abandon ourselves and enter into God's point of view, to give to Him, to please Him, and to be united with Him. This is where the gulf between charity and any other kind of love of God is so evident. The disciple of Jesus knows that he is loved by God, who is infinitely near to him, and his essential impulse is not to satisfy his capacity for desire, but to respond to the love wherewith he is loved. It is not a self-seeking, but a self-giving; it is not to satisfy himself, but to please God.

The Christian will thus be interested first of all in whatever touches God. If his prayer is praise and adoration, he will praise God for God's sake, and it will be

God's perfections and life that form the object of his gratification. If, on the other hand, it is a prayer of asking, it will ask for all that glorifies God; only afterward will it descend to particular requests.

Let it be remembered, also, that this is the prayer that Christ taught His people. The Our Father is the most perfect of prayer formulas and will always provide subject matter for commentaries that bring out its riches and applications; but it is also the ideal, the rule, the measure, the inspiration, and the model for all Christian prayers.

Our Father makes us aware of God's fatherhood and the infinite love that has adopted us in the Son, so that we are in truth His children. *Our* tells us that we stand in real relationship with all those whom God loves equally. In one gesture, Christ has snatched His own from any egotism, from any preoccupation with themselves, from any narrowness, from any confined human attitude, and has set them in the truth of the love that loves God filially and God's children fraternally.

Next, the requests we are to learn teach us to be busy with whatever touches God, and only subsequently to think about what touches ourselves.

Considered purely as an act of religion — that is to say, as the effort of man wanting to honor God — all prayer should have this characteristic of self-neglect and of free sacrifice. When we consider it as the working of the gift of piety, it goes farther still; moved by the Spirit, it takes on a divine nature and a divine dimension. The Angelic Doctor expressed it with eternally fresh aptness: "A gift such as the gift of piety is for the honor of God, but the gift has a divine manner and a divine measure. It pays honor to God, not because we owe it to Him, but because He is worthy of it in Himself. This manner is that in which God holds Himself in honor."[25] To understand it is to love, is to look for God alone and His pleasure, and thus become one with Him.

This concern to give to God and to draw near to Him for Himself does not exclude or disqualify any other motives, but it puts them in their proper perspective and gives them their full meaning in the great current of love.

It is natural to pray when we are shouting from the bottom of an abyss and we are as sure of God as a sentry is sure of the dawn. It is natural, also, to fly to Him for refuge, as in the psalm that has been the delight of so

---

[25] St. Thomas Aquinas (1225-1274; Dominican philosopher and theologian), *In III. Dist.* 34, Q. 3, art. 2, q. 1, ad. 1.

many generations of Christians: "He that dwelleth in the aid of the Most High shall abide under the protection of the God of Jacob. He shall say to the Lord: 'Thou art my protector and my refuge; my God, in Him will I trust.' "[26] It is normal to desire Him with a panting desire "as the hart panteth after the fountains of water."[27] Finally, it is natural to look for guidance in the words of God that must guide and judge our lives. But all these are component parts of the dialogue between created love, which has been given all and has expected all, and infinite love, whose glory it is to give.

Arising as it does from love, Christian prayer must tend toward loving and nothing else, since there is no other means of attaining to the divine union. It can lead to this in many ways. It makes it possible to gain knowledge of Christ's charity "that you may be filled unto all the fullness of God";[28] it shows the forms this love will take in daily life, thus becoming a response to "If God hath so loved us . . .";[29] it will coincide with God's views

[26] Ps. 90:1-2 (RSV = Ps. 91:1-2).
[27] Ps. 41:2 (RSV = Ps. 42:1).
[28] Eph. 3:19.
[29] 1 John 4:11.

and share in His intentions. St. Teresa speaks of it thus: "The important thing is not to think much, but to love much. Perhaps we do not know what it is to love, and I should not be much surprised at that. He who loves most is not he who receives the most consolations, but he who is the most resolute in pleasing God in everything, in doing more for the honor and glory of His Son, as for the exaltation of the Catholic Church."[30]

✣

Rely on love, not on methods of prayer

In one way or another, love is always sacrifice and self-abandonment, so that prayer must be characterized by putting ourselves completely at the disposal of the divine working. "The secret of secrets in prayer is to follow its attractions in great simplicity of heart," says St. Francis de Sales. It will be distinguished also by the absence of verbiage and convention, and will thus remain genuine. "True love hath but little method," but its bent will be toward all that will deepen it. In fact, it is good to be sparing with words and to cling to one word or

---

[30] St. Teresa of Avila, *The Castle of the Soul,* Fourth Mansion, ch. 1.

another — "a little word of one syllable . . . secretly meant in the depth of the spirit,"[31] which is, in the opinion of the author of *The Cloud of Unknowing*, worth more than an entire psalter. "Study thou not about words," he says, "for so shouldst thou never come to thy purpose, nor to this work, for it is never gotten by study, but only by grace."

St. Catherine[32] insists on the importance for spiritual progress of "welcoming the Lord's visits." St. Ignatius also recommends it: "If the person considering the Lord's Prayer find in one or two of the words good matter for thought, and spiritual relish, and consolation, he should not be anxious to pass on, even though the hour be spent on that one word which he has found. . . ."[33]

In this light, it is clear how vast a distance lies between our reading, our reflection, the formulas we use, and this ascension that is true prayer. To all of these elements used in prayer, whether to a greater or lesser extent, we could apply the exposition of true prayer in

---

[31] *The Cloud of Unknowing*, chs. 37-39.

[32] St. Catherine of Siena (1347-1380), Dominican tertiary.

[33] St. Ignatius of Loyola (1491-1556; founder of the Society of Jesus), *Spiritual Exercises*, no. 254.

one of Tauler's sermons: "Reading and vocal prayer sometimes serve toward this upstirring, and, as such, it may be praiseworthy to make use of them. Just as my cloak and my clothes are useful to me although they are not myself, so vocal prayer may be of service to real prayer, still without being it; it is the spirit and the heart that must go to God without intermediary. It is solely that and nothing else that is the essence of true prayer. The rising of the spirit to God through love, the inward and humble submission to God: this only is true prayer."[34]

It emerges clearly from these principles that the value of any prayer depends, not on an artificial attitude, but on the reality of the life of the soul. The great Christian mystics all agree that questions of spiritual hygiene, of temperament, of silence, of study, or of intellectual capacity are less important than moral progress, the development of virtues in the soul that are charity's imprint and become a closer and closer assimilation to Christ. St. Thomas said this, summing up all the wisdom of the Fathers: "The moral virtues belong to

[34] Jean Tauler (1300-1361; Dominican preacher and mystic), Extract from a sermon in preparation for Pentecost, Tome II, 22.

contemplation in the capacity of preliminary predispo-sitions"[35] St. Teresa restated it, and appealed to her own experience: "Never forget this important truth: the only thing that those who begin to give themselves up to prayer must be prepared for is to labor. They must be ready to conform their will to the will of God, coura-geously and by all possible means. Be well assured that in this consists, as I shall show from what is to follow, the most sublime perfection to which anyone can rise in the spiritual path. The more one practices this confor-mity, the more one receives from God, and the more one progresses in this way also. Do not go thinking that there are other secrets or other unknown and extraordi-nary methods of progressing; all our good is there."[36]

⚶

Avoid self-seeking in your prayer

By thus putting Christian prayer into its relation with charity, and showing it as the very expression and the food of charity, two of the dangers that threaten it

---

[35] St. Thomas Aquinas, *Summa Theologica*, II-II, Q. 180, art. 2.

[36] *The Castle of the Soul*, Second Mansion.

are at once removed: either to regard it as a work that can successfully be achieved by mere technique or proficiency, or to seek in it a personal gratification by more or less consciously pursuing a spiritual experience.

To make a labor of prayer is radically to falsify its nature, for, instead of our giving ourselves to God, it makes us take up an attitude that in no way interests Him who is Truth; it places prayer in the ranks of possession and human wealth, which cannot be part of the union with God. Certainly legislative wisdom, and in individual cases the prudence of confessors, recommends a certain time for prayer, but this span of time measured by the clock is intended to help everyone to attain the inward quality which is all that is of value in these matters.

As for the self-seeking in which a person more or less consciously pursues — perhaps even sheltering under the use of God's name — a spiritual experience and an inward satisfaction, this is a gangrene that threatens all spiritual people and from which only a very pure love can save them. "He that loveth me shall be loved of my Father; and I will love him and will manifest myself to him."[37] It is a matter of loving, and of doing what pleases

[37] John 14:21.

Christ, and it is He who manifests Himself. Or, rather, it is because of this unity of will achieved by the love of Him that the Father loves this friend of His Son, and Father and Son together come to dwell in such a friend.

⚜

Let your prayer spring from love
and lead to acts of love

Finally, two important points: first, prayer in its true worth is thus both pre-eminent and at the same time subsidiary: pre-eminent, because it is an affair of love; subsidiary, because it is for this love, and from it alone, that prayer, like the other realities of Christian life, derives all its value. Love does not exist for contemplation; contemplation exists for love.

The second point is the obvious emptiness of the reproach sometimes brought against prayer, that it hinders action, keeps people away from men's sufferings, and detaches them from their urgent responsibilities. If prayer is genuine, and if it is love, it must bring people nearer to God, and nearer to His children and their sufferings and aspirations. The prayer that cleaves to God because it loves Him, and desires to increase that love, automatically removes all contemporary misinterpretations, since it is shown to be the only response to the Christian ideal. Nobody who accosts God through love can be in any danger of forgetting that which God loves; he will present his brothers to God; and then, when he returns to action, he will be nearer to them and to their cares, because he will have grown in love. Contemplation, then, is not a subtraction from the active side of life, but an addition to it.

❧

Make prayer a priority

Before repeating yet again what spiritual authors have reiterated ever since they began to write about prayer as a separate subject, it is necessary to say that prayer is a function of the Church. When the eye sees or the ear hears, it is the whole body that is seeing and hearing through its organs; when the Christian prays, he prays as part of the whole Church. This truth, so important to the Christian, throws light on the part that contemplatives play in the life of the Church; but it is also a reminder that prayer is not an optional duty, but one of vital importance for the Church and one whose omission harms more than oneself.

Tauler pictured those who prayed as "the pillars of the world," without whom it would collapse; St. John of the Cross phrased the value of this function of the life with God unforgettably when he said, "A little of this pure love, although it appears to do nothing, is more precious before God and before the soul, and more profitable to the Church, than all other works put together."[38]

Are we sufficiently conscious of our responsibility in this matter of prayer — its quality even more than its length? Prayer can obtain whatever God is willing to give, not only for ourselves, but for His whole kingdom. It is often said that "a soul that rises lifts the world." When does it lift it higher than when rising toward God in prayer?

A Christian should never forget that, like the Apostles, he has been appointed "to bring forth fruit," and to obtain from the Father whatever he asks in the name of Christ.[39] How can he ignore this obligation? How can he forget it when he sees the coming of the Holy Spirit prepared for by the prayer of Mary, the Mother of Jesus? The Church, where it is permanently Pentecost, asks that prayer should be equally permanent.

[38] St. John of the Cross, *Cant.*, Second compilation, str. 28.

[39] Cf. John 15:16.

Make prayer a priority

Let prayer deepen your personality

It is particularly important nowadays to insist on this obligation of prayer by and for the community, to eliminate misunderstanding, which tends to discredit it and class it among personal, and even "individualistic" affairs. Of course it is, of all human activities, the most personalizing: those moments, lost to outward and visible usefulness, but consecrated to God's glory, are the most useful to man himself. And their value increases in proportion to their disinterestedness. He who thinks only of giving, receives; he who seeks only to glorify God is himself exalted, enlarged, developed, and strengthened. Prayer introduces us to the very heart of the mystery; it makes us reborn of the love wherein he who loses his life saves it and wherein a man possesses God to the same degree that he has abandoned himself.

The modern expression for this benefit of a living relationship with God is its "personalizing" character. A being's personality consists both in his unity and his accessibility, his inwardness and his power of communicating himself. Personality requires both an inward solidarity and a detachment from external conditions. Now, it is only in God that the creative source of personality is to be found; there is nothing that can so rouse a being, integrate him, detach him from the unessential, make him receptive, and broaden him as much as his relations with God, of person to Person, and of spirit to Spirit. The fact that in so many Christians there is an all-too-obvious lack of personality, an absence of concern for their responsibilities, that there is narrowness among them, and strife, is an indictment of the adequacy of their prayer.

By prayer, the soul places itself in a position to be re-created as it was first created; it receives its fulfillment from Him who gave it existence; it comes to rest in the pentecostal spring and in the fire of love, as it was born of the Spirit. Its life is set in Christ, as it were, to the beat and rhythm of the Father.

By making us conscious of our creation and our adoption, prayer makes us share in Christ's intentions and virtues. Without it, ideas — even those taught by the Faith — remain external, unassimilated, and distant; but with it they become living and personal and, as it were, experienced.

To give some idea of the gap between the theoretical and the experienced, Fr. Lallemant, speaking of Hell, said that this gap was as great as the difference between a painted lion and a real lion. St. Teresa used the description of an "instructed man": "A man who does not pray is like a paralyzed or crippled body, which has hands and feet but cannot use them."[40]

It is, of course, only gradually that our desires, born of faith, will turn into the reality of our feelings and permeate our thoughts and actions. Such permeation is brought about largely through the silence of prayer. The lukewarmness of our lives and the futility of so many of our good resolutions clearly show that we do not know how to keep quiet and listen, that we have not thought sufficiently to ask or to receive.

It is when we have learned this that prayer becomes the source of the greatest good, the meeting place where we think of nothing but God and of meeting Him who "speaks face-to-face, as a man is wont to speak to his friend."[41] This is how prayer creates genuine apostles, people who acquire from Christ a tormenting anxiety for the salvation of the world, although a short time before, the same people thought of nothing but themselves. "The soul in this state is just like wax on which

[40] *The Castle of the Soul*, First Mansion.
[41] Exod. 33:11.

Christ prints His seal; it is not the wax that imprints itself; it is merely prepared ready to receive it."[42]

Only through continued conversation with Christ, and through being His companion, do we learn to be His envoy, to do what He wants us to do, and to do it in His way. Words carry weight if they pass through God. "This virtue would not have been produced if the superior had not been talking to God," as St. Gregory of Nyssa[43] said of Moses. Prayer, more than a friend's counsels and better than our own heart, binds us to God's wisdom.

"But be continually with a holy man, whomsoever thou shalt know to observe the fear of God, whose soul is according to thy own soul; and who, when thou shalt stumble in the dark, will be sorry for thee. And establish within thyself a heart of good counsel; for there is no other thing of more worth to thee than it. The soul of a holy man discovereth sometimes true things; more than seven watchmen that sit in a place to watch. But above all these things, pray to the Most High, that He may direct thy way in truth."[44]

---

[42] *The Castle of the Soul*, Fifth Mansion.

[43] St. Gregory of Nyssa (c. 335-c. 395), bishop.

[44] Ecclus. 37:15-19 (RSV = Sir. 37:12-15).

Thus, it is not a question of using God for our own activities, but, on the contrary, of giving our activity to God as a sacrifice and lifting it right up to Him. It is not necessary for us to put an end to the worldly responsibilities that we have undertaken; simply laying them before God changes them into prayer. The fact of being drawn to Him by love draws all our burdens to God. That is why St. Thérèse of Lisieux was content to entreat, with the spouse of the Canticle of Canticles, "Draw me . . ." knowing that all else would follow: "In drawing me, Jesus, you will draw the souls that I love."[45]

⚜

Don't let lack of time or ability
keep you from praying

But if a reminder of the need for prayer is an opportunity for once more asserting its value, this does not answer the objections in so many people's minds. "I haven't the time." "I cannot pray." One reply answers both. The very necessity of prayer proves that it is possible. God, eager to give to every one of His people,

[45] Cf. St. Thérèse of Lisieux (1873-1897; Carmelite nun), *Story of a Soul*, ch. 11.

solicitous to save the world by the help of those who co-operate with His love, cannot offer impossible means, for then they would not be means but obstacles, no longer a call but a rejection. That would run counter to His wisdom as much as to His love.

People excuse themselves by saying they have no time, but even if someone does not have half an hour, he may have three times ten minutes or even ten times three minutes. Anyone busy from morning until night usually has sometimes a spare moment during the morning or the evening; he can probably escape from time to time, as the Master showed how, either in the morning, before the day's work, or at night. The Master withdrew to the desert for a moment to procure a little peace for His disciples, who no longer had time to eat: "Come apart into a desert place, and rest a little."[46] Besides, if time is really lacking, the will to pray *is* prayer — and an excellent one, provided that it really is a true will. The will to pray counts more than the length of the prayer. It is this will that pleases God, because it is love, and it can make up for all impossibilities; it will seize opportunities and, if necessary, create them.

[46] Mark 6:31.

As for inability, it is founded on a misapprehension. Here again, God does not ask the impossible; it is men who have complicated the issue. God is near, and there is no one who cannot talk to Him, love Him, and confide in Him. St. Thérèse of Lisieux explains what she means by *prayer*: "For me, prayer is a flight of the heart; it is simply a look cast toward Heaven; it is a cry of gratitude and love in the midst of trials as in the midst of joy. In short, it is something great and supernatural, which expands my soul and unites me to Jesus."[47]

Even more simply, Charles de Foucauld[48] received this definition of prayer from the Master within him: "To pray is to think of me while loving me." And who cannot do this?

---

[47] *Story of a Soul*, ch. 10.

[48] Charles de Foucauld (1858-1916), French army officer who became a hermit in Palestine.

✣

Learn to overcome difficulties in prayer

Every part of a Christian's life must be "worthy of God," but this obligation is felt most in the realm of prayer and direct relations with God. This is why the difficulties of prayer seem greater, and why it is so easily neglected. Some of these difficulties — such as routine, artificiality, the burden of the human estate, distraction, and false trends — are too great to be passed over in silence.

The power that has been entrusted to men is astounding to the point of stupefaction; it allies men to omnipotence. "If you ask the Father anything in my name, He will give it to you."[49] St. Paul could assert,

[49] John 16:23.

"Godliness is profitable to all things, having promise of the life that now is and of that which is to come."[50]

⚜

Be mindful of whom you address in prayer

It is a great mystery to speak to God and to be able, in our earthly lifetime, to converse with Him when He is in Heaven. Familiarity blinds us to the marvelous and solemn nature of this divine reality. Those who have had the grace of a Christian education learned to speak to God as soon as they learned to speak to men; they entered into conversation with their Father in Heaven even before they had time to be astonished at the boldness of such an undertaking. And because this very familiarity with God can make us lose the sense of its reality, we must constantly meditate on the great value of prayer, considering how the Father counts it as being of great worth, how He looks for it, and considering the great place it occupies in all Scripture, especially in the Gospels. Jesus taught us to pray, and we have to place ourselves in such a state of receptiveness that His teachings find a new and a willing soul.

[50] 1 Tim. 4:8.

Learn to overcome difficulties in prayer

It is important to begin every prayer very carefully, remembering whom we are addressing; prayer can never be words and gestures addressed to no one, words that are unheard even by the speaker, and are empty of thought and feeling. So we must first of all consider seriously to whom we are going to speak, and for what reason. The Sign of the Cross, taught by the Church from the earliest centuries, is a simple reminder of this.

❧

Avoid artificiality in your prayer

Moreover, prayer is a grace to be asked for: "We know not what we should pray for as we ought; but the Spirit Himself asketh for us with unspeakable groanings."[51] The battle against sticking in the rut of routine demands a ceaseless vigilance to keep our eyes open for realities as yet unseen.

Some people, however, reacting against this routine negligence, go to the other extreme. They think to live the grandeur of prayer by making of it something artificial and conventional. They fall back on thinking about the state of their souls, concerned more about their own

[51] Rom. 8:26.

prayer than about God. They concentrate on filling up the set time as conscientiously and as methodically as possible with a diligence that they call prayer, instead of understanding that a part of time was set aside to teach them how to pray all the time.

St. Teresa railed against those who are at pains to take up a motionless attitude, and hold their breath, concerned with themselves to the point of "not daring to stir": "How can they rejoice in the glory of God and desire its increase when they are thinking only of preventing their understanding from working?"[52] And at the other extreme, we can quote the great maxim of St. Anthony,[53] one of the patriarchs of the contemplative life, who declared prayer to be perfect only when the monk is no longer aware either of himself or of his prayer.

In prayer, more than in any other action, what is important is honesty, which prevents affectation in words or feeling and anything artificial in attitude or thought. Everywhere and always God looks toward the heart, but in this case, the heart shows itself to Him. Diligence and

---

[52] *The Castle of the Soul,* Fourth Mansion.

[53] St. Anthony (251-356), desert monk and father of Western monasticism.

striving will be directed, not toward setting up an attitude, but toward becoming completely true in love and in sorrow, genuinely ready to "be taught of God."[54]

It was one of the teachings of Christ that His disciples should pray withdrawn in their rooms, under the gaze of the Father, who sees in secret, and avoid the "much speaking" that would be the equivalent of a false attitude; for "your Father knoweth what is needful for you before you ask Him."[55] Ready-made methods and formulas are intended only to help achieve the frankness and transparence that gives us entirely to God.

We must, indeed, understand what we are talking about. What do we mean when we speak of praying well? Too often people are thinking of an abstract ideal, of an impulse, or of a rest for the senses. The best prayer is that which pleases God by its total surrender to Him; an offering to Him of a soul in which He may "reflect all that He is and do all that He wills."[56]

"The best prayer," says Bossuet, "is that in which one studies with more simplicity and humility to conform to

[54] John 6:45.

[55] Matt. 6:8.

[56] Sr. Elizabeth of the Trinity, *Last Retreat*.

the will of God and to the example of Jesus Christ, that in which one abandons oneself most to the dispositions and impulses that God puts into the heart by His grace and by His Spirit."

Prayer is a conversation with God, and the essential thing in all conversation is sincerity, in the person spoken to and in the speaker, in what is said and in the manner in which it is said. And because God is Spirit, "the speech which He loves is the silence of love."

Affectation can come from a good will badly taught, straining rather than giving and forgetting self, or from a self-absorption that thinks of self, of its own impressions, and of its own good works in God's sight, like the Pharisee when he reckoned up his deserts.[57] In either case, it brings a lack of truthfulness and thus creates an obstacle. God's "communication is with the simple."[58]

⚜

Preserve your intention to please God
Yet the man who wishes to pray meets other difficulties arising from his state, since he is flesh as well as

[57] Cf. Luke 18:11-12.
[58] Prov. 3:32.

spirit, and is influenced by the state of his nerves, his health, and the world outside him.

Let us first repeat categorically that no circumstance of tiredness, of inability, or of any external disturbance can prevent our yes to God, which makes any such circumstance an occasion for prayer. Mental attention may be impossible, concentration of thought may be unattainable, but it is always in man's power to give himself to God and to acquiesce (even in the anguish of anxiety) in the will of God. And normal daily impediments, whether tiredness or sleepiness or illness, are obstacles only at the human and conscious level of prayer; the man who clings to God's will through them will find an opportunity for rising above self to surrender to God.

St. Francis de Sales wrote to a lady who was lamenting that she could not pray: "My very dear daughter, we must not be unfair; when we are unwell in body and in health, we must demand of our spirit only acts of submission and holy uniting of our will to God's good pleasure. As for external actions, we must try to perform them as best we can, even if it be sluggishly; and to lift this listlessness and torpor of heart and make them of service to the divine love, we must acknowledge, accept, and love holy abjectness; thus you will change your leaden weight into fine gold."

As for distractions, the answer of the Curé d'Ars[59] is well known: flies settle on water only when it is tepid and do not approach it when it boils. A true love never becomes distracted, for it is thinking always of the beloved.

But this is not a completely simple problem, because the love of God, since it does not belong to the order of realities perceived by the senses, does not take hold of imagination or memory, and therefore distractions remain possible, and even inevitable, throughout the whole of life. St Thomas's answer to this is that involuntary distractions do not diminish the merit of prayer, but they hinder its fruits. In other words, the essential value of a prayer is not diminished by distractions. God looks to the heart — that is to say, the intention. Under the distracted mind He sees the intention to please Him, to cleave to Him, and to surrender to Him.

On the other hand, the fruits of prayer, the consolation it affords, the lamps it replenishes, and the rest in

---

[59] Curé d'Ars (1786-1859), St. John Vianney, patron saint of parish priests.

God that man's spirit finds are destroyed by these alien and tiring thoughts. Basically, it is of little importance, since God has lost nothing, so to speak, and only man is conscious of the loss, so that if distractions are endured in Christ's spirit, they remain one of the trials that make up a sharing in the Cross. Furthermore, almost any distraction can become an invitation to pray for something; what God wants is the intention of love that seeks only His glory.

"The effects of prayer," says St. Thomas, "are three in number. The first is common to all acts informed by charity: this is merit. To have this, it is not necessary for the attention to accompany the prayer from beginning to end; but by virtue of the initial intention, the entire prayer is rendered meritorious.

"The second effect, which belongs properly to prayer, is the intention (imperative efficacy). There again the first intention, which God looks at before anything else, is enough; if it is deficient, the prayer has neither merit nor efficacy for being granted. For God, says St. Gregory, does not listen to prayer made to Him without endeavor.

"Prayer has a third effect, which it produces in the soul by its very presence. It is a certain spiritual reflection, and this requires of necessity an attentive prayer. 'If my tongue alone prays, my spirit gathers no fruit.' "[60]

⚜

Beg God for the grace of prayer

The last difficulty we must discuss comes from a conflict between the spontaneity necessary for prayer and the awareness of an experience that demands help. It is clear, on the one hand, that prayer is an entirely personal affair, like love, like all acts in which men are involved; how can we help feeling repugnance at introducing any sort of arbitrary element into a soaring upward that derives its sole value from its spontaneity? On the other hand, it is impossible not to feel this need for help in the face of setbacks and uncertainties.

Since prayer is a grace, we must never cease to beg for it and to attach more importance to the merciful gift of the Lord than to our own strivings. "In vain," said Fr. Lallemant, "do we strive to have the presence of God unless He Himself gives it to us."[61] Yet the Lord wants

---

[60] *Summa Theologica*, II-II, Q. 83, art. 13.

[61] Fr. Lallemant, *Doctrine Spirituelle*, Fifth principle, ch. 2.

both our own effort and a willingness to find out from others what can help us. If prayer is to be spontaneous and genuine, it is essential that its spontaneity be directed by faith, for, as St. Francis de Sales tells us, "one hour of well-regulated devotion is worth more than a hundred days of outlandish melancholy depending on the brain."

It would be dangerous to trust to feeling in a matter that rises above it, and to forget that this world of liberty can lead to progress, and yet can also expose us to the risk of sliding back. It is left in man's hands to make himself or lose himself, but in the last analysis, it is not man who is the measure and the rule in this, but God. It is with regard to God that we need instruction, not so much from those who repeat His teaching as from Christ Himself, the sole Master, who prays in us. "He is the mouth without deceit through whom the Father has spoken in truth."[62]

[62] St. Ignatius of Antioch (d. c. 107; disciple of John the Evangelist, bishop, and martyr), *Letter to the Romans*.

Chapter Four

ॐ

Learn the elements of perfect prayer

How are we to pray? To this question St. Francis de Sales replied in a letter: "True love has little method" — a principle that did not, however, prevent him from expounding at length some wise and stimulating advice on the best manner of praying, or from devoting an entire section of his *Introduction to a Devout Life* to this subject.

It is important to emphasize again that since prayer is a meeting of person with person, it is a living reality, and it would be illusory to imagine it as discovered once and for all, or to believe that at any given moment, it should exclude certain patterns. Souls that are most guided by the Holy Spirit know that nothing in prayer comes ready-made. Starting from a pattern in which man's own effort seems to predominate, it tends, through becoming gradually more and more at God's disposal, to be increasingly influenced by the working and unifying control of the Holy Spirit. It is governed at first by human ideas, enlightened by faith, but it will take its ideal and its measure more and more from God's tastes and from His loving presence.

⚜

Compose yourself and think of God

All the spiritual masters seem to agree in recommending an approach to prayer by relaxation in calmness of mind and nerves, and in full awareness. Among others, St. Ignatius in his *Spiritual Exercises* expresses it thus: "Before entering on prayer, let the mind repose a little, and sitting or walking, according as shall seem best to me, I will think whither I am going, and for what purpose."[63] As long ago as the earliest Fathers, Origen insisted on this preparation and desired "that one should, as it were, stretch out one's soul before one's hands."[64]

---

[63] St. Ignatius of Loyola, *Spiritual Exercises*, no. 239.

[64] Origen (c. 185-253; Alexandrian writer and theologian), *Of Prayer*.

Learn the elements of perfect prayer

Then the disciple must put himself "in the fullness of faith" for this conversation with God; he will think of the love into which he is entering, of the "living and true God" to whom he is speaking. It is impossible to insist too much on the endeavor to set ourselves thus in the truth, for on it depends one of the essential benefits of prayer: that of being always with God. The length of time and the concentration given to the prayer help to put us in a truthful relation with God. Prayer is not an exercise, and life divorced from God is not real life. Prayer must be true if the whole of life is to be true. God is just as near, as attentive, and as loving throughout the whole day and night as He is at the actual times of prayer; the more intense moments are there to help us to discover the reality of always praying. Prayer must become so true that it makes life itself true, and renders it worthy of God. It will be useful and fruitful only if it is devoted entirely to putting ourselves in God's presence and offering ourselves to His love.

⚘

Meditate on the Gospel

It would appear that people are wise in objecting to the use of books during prayer, which all too often are used only as a means of avoiding effort; but it would be disastrous to confuse the Gospel with books written by men. For many, the Gospel is the means of entry into the divine intimacy and wisdom. It was the method dear to the ancients. "One hears Him, when reading; one speaks to Him when praying." Only one condition is necessary: this reading of the divine word, whether read in the book or in the heart, must really be a listening to Christ, receiving from His lips and His heart the words handed down to us.

It is interesting, on this subject, to read what a great Carthusian once said of the life of prayer. He shows how different forms are united and linked, comparing them to a ladder on which we can climb from earth to Heaven: "Reading looks for the unspeakable sweetness of the blessed life, prayer asks for it, and contemplation savors it. It is the very saying of the Lord, 'Seek and ye shall find. Knock and it shall be opened to you.' Seek by reading, and you will find by meditation. Knock by prayer, and you will enter by contemplation. I would like to say that reading carries the nourishing food to the mouth, meditation masticates and chews it, prayer tastes it, and contemplation is the sweetness itself that rejoices and restores."

Christ on one's forehead" and concentrating on Him the whole effort of the intelligence to try to understand His thoughts and Himself as a person; in one's heart, to try to love Him and to respond in desire, awe, or hope, according to the mood of the meditation; and finally, on one's arm, in order to perceive the practical application of the ideal and transfer it to life and action.

This is a very natural method suited to the human mind, which has first to grasp, understand, and reflect on these ideas which are going to strengthen love, and develop resolutions that must be put into effect in active life. It would be a mistake to think that fulfillment begins only at the end of prayer, for, since all prayer is a relation with God, it must produce sacrifice, love, and acquiescence in God's good pleasure. A single genuine act of love is enough to make us exist in God, and there is nothing greater; it will transform the whole routine of daily life.

At this point, the imagination has its place in the effort to grasp Christ. St. Francis de Sales says, "And for that, if you did some violent imagining, no doubt you needed to correct it; but if you make it brief and simple, merely a means to recall your mind to attention, I do not think that it is as yet necessary to leave it altogether.

Imaginings must be simple and very short, for they ought to be used only as a mere passage from distraction to recollection."[66]

Imagination can serve to make the divine realities felt in the senses and to root such feelings in the Gospels. It can help in grasping the real nature of the happenings in the earthly life of our Lord. But imagination must not be a stopping point, for only faith can attain to the divine reality. Too much imagination has its own drawbacks, for if we remain at this level, the resulting emotion is superficial and often misleading. St. Ignatius insists on the need for passing quickly from the evangelical scene to the divine mystery.

❧

Pray in faith, hope, and charity

Others prefer to start from the structure of the supernatural system, and do all their praying in faith, hope, and charity. Faith cleaves to God's mystery, either in Himself or in one of the aspects under which He has revealed Himself to us. Hope expects God from God and,

---

[66] St. Francis de Sales, *On Imagination and Understanding,* June 8, 1606.

according to individual cases, aspires to meet Him face-to-face, or else derives security from His help. Charity is united to God. This prayer leaves everything to God as He is present in us; it exposes our intelligence to His mystery, surrenders us to His action, and comes to rest in Him and for Him. It clings in the present to God, who is present, whether it rests in God's mystery, or whether it receives Him through one of His sayings or one of His approaches, His works, or His gifts.

Some people react so much against "reasoned" methods that they make the mistake of being overly emotional. Disliking exaggerated rationalism, they do not thirst sufficiently for the wisdom that is communion with God's thoughts.

St. Francis de Sales warned St. Jane de Chantal against such extremes: "As for the precepts of prayer, I shall say nothing about them at present; but to take as one's rule not to prepare oneself seems to be a little hard, as also to come out of God's presence without thanksgiving, without offering, or any particular prayer. All this can be done usefully."[67]

---

[67] St. Francis de Sales to St. Jane de Chantal (1572-1641; foundress of the Visitation Order), March 11, 1610.

Learn the elements of perfect prayer

✣

Pray with attention and devotion

In conclusion, we must mention a piece of advice that is common to all authors who have treated of prayer — that is, we should recite every prayer or psalm slowly, concentrating as profoundly as possible on the meaning.

St. Thérèse of the Child Jesus gives her own experience: "Sometimes my spirit is in so great a dryness that it is impossible for me to draw from it one thought to unite me to God; I recite very slowly an Our Father and then a Hail Mary; then these prayers enrapture me; they feed my soul much more than if I had recited them quickly a hundred times."[68]

It is clear that God desires to unite Himself to His children, and to bless them by making them like Him, infinitely more than they can desire it themselves. It is also clear that this union of love cannot be realized at the level of man, with his spiritual egotism, his emotions, and his ideas, but only at God's level. This is why the end of man's prayer is to be at God's disposal to

[68] Original manuscript of St. Thérèse of Lisieux, folio 25.

renounce everything, including his own self, to lay himself open to God, and to let himself be drawn toward "all truth,"[69] so realizing the supreme desire of Christ: to be in us so that we live in Him.

[69] John 16:13.

Chapter Five

Address God as
your loving Father

This book is not concerned merely with praying, but with praying well. Everything in the ideal and the laws governing prayer was changed when the Son first spoke to the Father in the language of men, and when the Son's Spirit entered the hearts of the adopted children and made them cry out, "Abba, Father."[70] Everything changed; everything is new, and it is now impossible to speak to God without entering into this new situation.

But how can we talk of newness when the Church still uses the Old Testament expressions? The answer is very simple: "He has brought all newness in bringing

---

[70] Gal. 4:6.

Himself."[71] Everything is new because He has come. The words do not change, but the facts they describe do. The reality of prayer is different because Christ has come into the world and has sent it His Spirit.

Yet a first superficial search seems to bring disappointing results. What do we know of Christ's prayer? The Gospels tell us of solitary prayer far into the night or before the dawn; and they tell of the thanksgiving that became a miracle.[72] But what more do we know?

There is — and it is infinitely sufficient — the fact that Christ calls God *Father,* and that He is the Son, having all in common with the Father. "All things are delivered to me by my Father";[73] "All my things are Thine, and Thine are mine";[74] "What shall I say? . . . Father, glorify Thy name."[75] He acquiesces in His will as in an absolute; when He speaks to God of His executioners, He speaks as one possessing God's justice and mercy, and He abandons Himself to Him.

---

[71] St. Hilary.

[72] Cf. Luke 6:12; John 6:9-14.

[73] Matt. 11:27.

[74] John 17:10.

[75] John 12:27, 28.

Address God as your loving Father

Every time Christ speaks to God, He calls Him *Father*, because He is the Son. When, in His last prayer, he uses a verse from the Psalms, everything in it becomes new, because he substitutes the name *Father* for *Jehovah*: "Father, into Thy hands I commend my spirit!"[76] There is only one exception: once, on the Cross. Christ takes for His own the psalmist's heart-rending cry and addresses it to God, who has abandoned Him.[77] Is it His will to express His cry of entreaty in the psalmist's own words and so to identify Himself with all human distress? Might it not also be the effort of redeeming love?

On the first day of His public life, in the Nazareth synagogue, Christ opened Isaiah at the page that gave meaning to the "this day" that was to be the beginning of His public life;[78] on the Cross, His heart-rending cry is intended to remind those who condemned Him, but whom He wishes to save, of the psalm that most explicitly prophesies the death and the redeeming fruitfulness of the Messiah. Whatever the explanation, the disciples

---

[76] Luke 23:46; cf. Ps. 30:6 (RSV = Ps. 31:5).

[77] "My God, my God, why hast Thou forsaken me?" (Matt. 27:46; cf. Ps. 21:2 [RSV = Ps. 22:1]).

[78] Luke 4:21.

who repeated the cry certainly took refuge in the yea of the Garden of Olives in order to cling to the will of the Father, with whom nothing is impossible and who asks nothing except in love. We shall come back to this later.

Surely the "Yes, Father, because it is Thy will . . ." and "Father, glorify Thy name" are the most complete expressions of filial love. From them disciples are always learning to identify themselves with God's good pleasure and to think of nothing but His glory in time and in eternity.

The two longer prayers of our Lord, preserved by St. John, do not seem to add anything to the fullness of this simplicity. The first is the thanksgiving before the resurrection of Lazarus;[79] here the Son does not ask, for He knows that His demands are always granted, but He rejoices at something that will make the truth of His mission shine out. The other, much longer, is the great prayer that begins the Passion. The Son is concerned solely with the Father's glory, and He can call him only Father, holy Father: "Glorify Thy Son, that Thy Son may glorify Thee . . . that they may see my glory which

[79] John 11:41-42.

Thou hast given me, because Thou hast loved me."[80] It lets us share the Son's thoughts and introduces us to God's vast plan, of which we are part, but the filial attitude is the same. There is the same acknowledgment that everything belonging to the Father is the Son's, as everything of His belongs to the Father, the same entire absorption in the Father's glory.

❧

Imitate Christ's filial devotion

It is to this filial prayer that Christ wishes to introduce His people. But in order to make them realize the extreme distance between them and the position to which they are called by grace and adoption — a position that, far from being a personal privilege, is their bond with other men — He teaches them to say, "Our Father, who art in Heaven . . ." He never uses the word *heavenly* when He speaks to the Father for Himself, for He is not distant from Him; nor does He ever, for Himself, say *our*, but always *the Father* or *my Father*.

But allowing this distance, the filial love of the Son remains the ideal and the inspiration of disciples. The

[80] John 17:1, 24.

adoption is more real than all created descent; the relationship is an infinitely true one, and the other qualities of Christian prayer will follow from trust in the goodness of the best of fathers. "If thou, then, being evil, know how to give good gifts to your children; how much more will your Father who is in Heaven give good things to them that ask Him?"[81] Perseverance obtains unfailingly what it asks; it triumphs even over the laziness or neglect of men who are either unscrupulous or concerned wholly with themselves; the Lord does not hesitate to make the comparison between the unjust judge and the most holy Father.[82] Humility, above all, keeps a man in truth and procures mercy for him.

The content of prayer will always be entirely new, for, in becoming as a child, the disciple must inevitably set himself at God's point of view in order to exist in truth; he must concern himself pre-eminently with God's glory and with His kingdom, by abandoning himself to the will of the Father, who encompasses earth and Heaven. Finally, the disciple will learn how much the Father values this new adoration, for He seeks such adorers as

[81] Matt. 7:11.
[82] Luke 18:1-8.

these, and the Son does not hesitate to wear Himself out in order to find them: He "being wearied with His journey, sat thus on the well";[83] wearied with the journey from Judea to Galilee, but wearied even more by the path leading down from the Father's bosom to the human state. "Seeking me, You have sat wearied by Your search."[84]

[83] John 4:6.
[84] *Dies Irae*, v. 10.

ᵉ

Reflect on the Our Father

When a Christian withdraws to talk to the Father in secret, his prayer ought in one way or another to repeat the prayer Christ taught us: "Thus, therefore, shall you pray. . . ."[85] Everything in a disciple's life must be new, and his prayer, too, is always new. Christ drew this prayer from the fullness of His heart; He wishes to mold His disciple through His soul, in the most excellent of actions: conversation with God.

In St. Luke's Gospel, it was when Christ came back from praying that His followers asked His secret: "Lord, teach us to pray, as John also taught his disciples."[86] The

[85] Matt. 6:9.
[86] Luke 11:1.

context would appear to indicate that the form of the Our Father was the very one that our Lord Himself used — a relic more valuable than a piece of the true Cross, since it has arisen from the divine heart and from the most intimate depths of His soul. The Master teaches us all that we want, all that we need to ask.

The Our Father holds so great a place in the forming of the Christian mind that its delivery and recitation were surrounded with solemnity from the first moment of a catechumen's preparation for Baptism.

Father: A name of infinite love, love that is close and kind, giving all that can be given; personal love that has even numbered the hairs of our heads.[87] "Behold what manner of charity the Father hath bestowed upon us, that we should be called and should be the sons of God."[88]

Our: God is in truth none other than the Father of Him who is Brother to each and every man, and who is one with us.

In Heaven: The Father's house is the only place where God reveals Himself in all His reality, the only place where His love reaches its goal and can rest,

[87] Cf. Matt. 10:30.
[88] 1 John 3:1.

where "we shall be like to Him, because we shall see Him as He is."[89]

Hallowed be Thy name: To pray is to raise yourself to God, to take His point of view and enter into His interests. His glory, "to make Him known and loved," should be our passion. "I have glorified Thee on the earth."[90] "Hallowed be Thy name" is to say may His name, His personality, and His being never be confused with anything else, but be glorified and loved in a manner worthy of Him.

Thy kingdom come: All the good of time and of eternity, all that Christ has brought us, all God's interests, here and everywhere, now and always, His overwhelming presence in His people — may we desire it truly and ask for it in truth.

Thy will be done: On earth, in the clouds of faith and the darkness of trial, as in Heaven in the perfection of love, absolute abandonment and identification with God's good pleasure. "Yea, Father, for so hath it seemed good in Thy sight."[91] This demand ought to broaden us

[89] 1 John 3:2.
[90] John 17:4.
[91] Matt. 11:26.

and deepen us in proportion with all the vastness and perfection of His will.

Give us: Give us our needs now, but in relationship to Thee. "The bread," the food of our intelligence and heart and soul. "Not in bread alone doth man live, but in every word that proceedeth from the mouth of God."[92] And bread for the body today, today's bread. It is useless to make provision. Lacordaire[93] used to say to one of his friends, "Of tomorrow you know nothing except that Providence will get up for you earlier than the sun."

Forgive us: The forgiveness that goes so far as to forget and to make white what was scarlet;[94] that never tires, but begins afresh every day, as do our sins and our forgetfulness. All our life is wretched and waits on His mercy.

As we forgive: We would wish our forgiveness to be like His, but only He can grant us such a gift.

Lead us not into temptation: "Keep us as we keep the apple of our eye," which we value most while we know

---

[92] Matt. 4:4.

[93] Jean-Baptiste-Henri Dominique Lacordaire (1802-1861), French orator.

[94] Cf. Isa. 1:18.

how easily it can be broken beyond repair. And if trial should come, even if it is the sacrifice of Isaac,[95] let it be an opportunity for pure love, and may it increase our intimacy with Him!

Deliver us from evil: The only evil is what separates us from God; it is to love Him too little. "The only sadness is not to be like saints."[96]

Amen: Yes, *amen* to all that is God, and to all that He wishes to accomplish in us and outside us; to His whole will and to His grace, turning all to trust, fidelity, and adoration. May our whole being cleave to the purposes and demands of His love. May our soul and the entire earth open to receive what He wishes to give us!

[95] Cf. Gen. 22:1-2.
[96] Léon Bloy, *The Poor Woman*.

࿎

Chapter Seven

Adore God in
spirit and in truth

Christ's conversation with the Samaritan woman[97] is one of the peaks of Christian revelation on the subject of prayer; if it were possible to make a judgment on such a subject, we might call it the culmination. There is one sentence so significant as to leave us no rest: "For the Father also seeketh such to adore Him."[98] God, who is infinitely happy in Himself, and who is all good, looks for something: adoration. We might think that He lacked something, that something created might be to His taste, might correspond to what He is. The words of

[97] John 4.
[98] John 4:23.

the Old Testament suddenly appear in a new light: the metaphor "sacrifices of sweet odor," which had seemed exaggerated, used of the prayer that pleases God, has suddenly become true, because the search for God has taken human form, the form of Christ sitting on the ground near the well, asking the Samaritan woman for water. She stands and is unable to see in this Stranger, exhausted by His journey, the man who makes the inexhaustible waters flow. The exhaustion and the asking: here is God's quest for adoration.

Before going further, it is necessary to understand to whom the request is addressed. We might think it would be to some soul grown old in holiness, long withdrawn into the wilderness in preparation for hearing such a request, one of those men wise in meditation who guard the oldest secrets. But no, it is to a woman busy drawing water for her household, a woman who scoffs, is scornful and superficial, and who, furthermore, has reached her fifth lover! This is the person whom God seeks out, for whose adoration He asks.

By this manner of asking, He proclaims that He has come to seek what was dying; He reveals that His love is free; above all, He makes felt — and felt to be of indisputably universal application — the sublime doctrine that there is no sinner and no human soul that is not called to this intimate relationship with the Father.

⚶

Praise God for His majesty

Now let us try to understand this teaching and learn once and for all that living with God must be first of all living *for* God, and a cleaving to Him for His own sake.

What, then, is adoration? It is an attitude in which a sense of God is expressed and fulfilled; a sense of God as He is in Himself and of what He is in relation to us. It is, then, partly a marveling at what He is; we speak to Him of what He is, or better, we are silent because of what He is. It is a tremulous rejoicing, unable to express God, but also unable not to try to express Him.

"Adoration," says Sr. Elizabeth of the Trinity, "this is a word from Heaven. It seems to me that it could be defined as an ecstasy of love. It is love overwhelmed by the beauty, the strength, the immense grandeur of the Beloved. It falls into a sort of swoon, into a full, deep silence, the silence David spoke of when he cried out, 'Silence is Thy praise.' And it is the most beautiful of all praise, since it is the praise that is sung eternally in the bosom of the unchanging Trinity, and it is also the last effort of the soul as it overflows and can say no more."[99]

That human speech should address itself to God and speak to Him of the world is already something great; but human speech becomes greater still when it speaks to God of Himself. The Master speaks only of adoration to the Samaritan woman. It is the theme the angels, on Christmas night, sang to mankind, summoned to the great rejoicing at the birth of the Lord: "Glory to God in the highest!" Man is invited to give glory to God; he is to approach God, not only to petition Him, but also to pay his respects and to talk about himself with Him. This is what adoration is. It is the movement that prostrates man before his Creator, acknowledging that he owes all to His all-powerful and freely given love: "What shall I render to the Lord for all the things that He hath rendered to me?"[100] It is the joyful recognition of having received all from His love, of being no more than a word spoken by the lips of Him who speaks and whose word gives all, of receiving existence itself merely from God's infinite and freely given love.

[99] *Last Retreat.*
[100] Ps. 115:12 (RSV = Ps. 116:12).

Yet it would be a poor thing to stop short at the feeling of dependence, to praise God only because of what He is "for me." It would be still too little to abandon myself to Him, becoming "an offering of praise." Charity makes me take pleasure in God as He is to Himself and rejoice in God's own happiness.

Adoration is love resting in its Beloved and becoming utterly oblivious to everything else. Sometimes adoration will cling to one of the divine perfections, to power, wisdom, goodness; sometimes it will travel from one to the other; but most often it will be withdrawn in silence, clinging with all its being to God in His mystery. The seraphim's *Sanctus,* which the prophets were given grace to hear, the cries of the book of Revelation, make us understand that the great prayer of eternity will be like this. "We shall be like Him"; we shall have entered into His life and His joy, "seeing Him as He is."

On earth, such prayer is manifestly the peak where our thought cannot always remain, but which it continually climbs so as to live the paschal mystery, thus passing into God through Christ dead and risen. Often God's works tell of His perfections, and the contemplation of nature draws us toward the invisible beauty whose imprint it bears. More perfectly, men, with their great needs and with the grace they receive, reflect as in a mirror the glory of the Lord. Among them, the Blessed Virgin shows us more closely God, who chose her and who expresses Himself in her as His masterpiece of grace. But it is the face of Christ on which the divine glory shines that will draw us into the truest adoration, for He is the "Only Begotten of the Father, full of grace and truth. . . . And of His fullness we all received"[101] He is the very object of the Father's kindness.

Through faith, many disciples have trodden the path to Mount Tabor, and still more the path to Golgotha, for on earth there can be no more arresting revelation of love; they have learned with St. Albert the Great[102] "to pass from the wounds of humanity to the glory of divinity."

Yet Faith has told us about the very mystery of the life of God, One in Three, Father, Son, and Holy Spirit, so that "in confessing the true and everlasting Godhead, we shall adore distinction in persons, oneness in being, and equality in majesty."[103] Seventeenth-century

---

[101] John 1:14, 16.

[102] St. Albert the Great (c. 1200-1280), medieval theologian, philosopher, and scientist.

[103] Preface for the Mass of the Feast of the Most Holy Trinity.

French mystics delighted in worshiping God with all His creation, and with His Son, both in His human nature and also as He existed before His human birth, when He lived only in God's presence; sometimes they envisaged the time before all creation, when only God existed. "In the beginning was the Word. . . ."[104]

When Christ said that "no one knoweth the Son but the Father; neither doth anyone know the Father but the Son,"[105] He showed us something of the immensity of the mystery to which He introduced us; and in this is centered all our adoration. It is not enough to praise God through what we know of Him; we must adore Him because of what He is in Himself, which He alone knows.

If such heights seem unscalable, if we think of prayer as concerned only with our own affairs, it shows the weakness of our love; it does not alter the fact that we are meant to praise the glory of the Love that has adopted us. The *Magnificat*,[106] which the Church asks us to say so often, ought to open up horizons where our

[104]John 1:1.
[105]Matt. 11:27.
[106]Luke 1:46-55.

soul soars, rising to exalt the Lord and to tremble with joy in God.

ی

Understand the adoration
that God seeks from you

To show what such adoration ought to be, Christ reminds us that God is Spirit and is the Father. To say, "God is Spirit" is to assert the absolute transcendence of His divine nature, which has nothing in common with what is bodily, limited, perceptible, quantitative, or divisible. He is infinitely beyond our imagination and our ideas; whereas, for us, only what is material seems real and existent, we must understand that the Spirit is infinite reality and absolute existence.

God is also "the Father," who dispenses freely given love, the first principle, who is nearest to us and who calls us to receive all from Him and to enter into intimacy with Him. "Father" takes us deep into the mystery of the divine life in which God is Father by begetting His Son. This is why, even if they went beyond the literal sense, the early writers were right to see in this text an invitation to enter into the life of the Trinity and to adore God in the Holy Spirit and in Truth, which is the Word.

And what is this adoration that the Father so prizes, the worship "in spirit and in truth"?[107]

It would be wrong to see in it a condemnation of gestures and external ritual; Christ Himself lifted His eyes to Heaven, went to Jerusalem, and observed the precepts of the law; He prostrated Himself with His face on the ground, lifted His arms in blessing. Any gesture that gives expression to the soul corresponds to something in man's nature, and God approves of it.

But we cannot fail to see in "truth" the new conditions of being a Christian. Before Christ came, relationship with God was symbolic; now it is a reality; it is no longer the time of darkness, but of the brightness of day, for the Sun of Justice has risen on the world.

To worship in spirit, we have to overcome all illusions of the senses and the imagination, all inadequate ideas that we make for ourselves; we have to adore God as He is and dwell with Him in a living relationship of person to person. "Give yourself as you are to God as He is."[108] So worship in spirit means at the same time passivity and activity, the unity of a soul resolved in

[107]John 4:23.
[108]*The Cloud of Unknowing.*

simplicity, the repose and the total gift of a being who has risen above being divided or scattered and has passed out of the domain of created things to enter into the repose of God.

Yet these are imperfect ways of expressing what happens, for the Spirit is neither above nor inside; He is within Himself. This is what Sr. Elizabeth of the Trinity meant when she wanted to explain her dwelling in God. "Thus *Laudem Gloriae* has found its retreat, its beatitude, and the foretaste of Heaven where it begins its eternal life before being transferred to the holy Jerusalem. It is without emerging from there that it will live in the image of the immutable Trinity in an eternal present, adoring it always for its own sake and becoming, by a gaze that grows progressively simpler and more unitive, 'the splendor of His glory,' otherwise called the unceasing and glorious praise of His adorable perfections."[109]

God expresses Himself in the whole of creation, and, to make us understand this mystery, Scripture repeats over and over again that God speaks and every creature is made. Man, in his adoration, becomes like an echo repeating God to God by love. In Heaven it will be a

[109]*Last Retreat.*

perfect echo; God will tell Himself of Himself through His elect. On earth there is darkness, but man opens Himself to reflect God's glory. And above all, He takes Christ as the pattern for His *amen*, for his total adherence to God, his loving acquiescence in all that God is and all that He does. That is why the great good news at Christmas was sung by the angels as "Glory to God."

Prayer is never a question of knowledge or time; a simple uplifting of the heart is enough to enter into God's glory and rejoice in His being. He gives the initiative, as He is the ideal. The man who adores is not the center of the spiritual world, drawing God to Himself. On the contrary, he is engulfed by the abyss; it is not for him to start or to produce, but to enter into the mysterious activity of love.

Chapter Eight

ℐ

Say yes to all that God asks of you

A disciple of Christ, wanting to learn from Him how to pray, will meditate on his Master's teachings and strive even harder to enter into His soul. There he hears the words preserved in the Gospels: "Yea, Father, for so hath it seemed good in Thy sight."[110] The same prayer, in a desolate form, anxious unto death, was the basis of the Agony in the Garden. There cannot be a loftier or simpler prayer. It is within everyone's scope, since it is the basis of goodwill in beginners; and it becomes, in those more advanced in prayer, the silent adherence that sinks them in God's depths. This exultant yes, this *amen, alleluia* is the song of eternity.

[110]Matt. 11:26.

The yes looks at God as He is and changes everything, whether important or trivial, into an offering. It is charged, too, with the world's sins and its misery, ready to watch with Christ. The wayfarer worn out by his toil, the apostle anxious for the world's salvation, the Christian who knows God in the joy of His presence or in the anguish of His absence — each can say yes and repeat it again and again, although each time in a different tone. This yes unites us to all that is God, to all that He is and to all that He wills; it gives Him all our being, all our sufferings, all our desires.

✣

Accept all things
from God's generosity

The yes of created existence answers the Creator's *fiat* — "He that sendeth forth light and it goeth; and hath called it, and it obeyeth Him with trembling. And the stars have given light in their watches and rejoiced. They were called and they said: 'Here we are.' And with cheerfulness they have shined forth to Him that made them."[111]

[111] Bar. 3:33-35.

Péguy's version is this: "And God Himself, young and eternal, saw what a world is that says yes."[112]

Our final transformation in Christ must correspond to God's initiative in adopting us by giving us His life. "For God, who commanded light to shine out of darkness, hath shined in our hearts, to give the light of the knowledge of the glory of God, in the face of Christ Jesus."[113] The yes of created fidelity fulfills the purposes of uncreated generosity. The Annunciation proclaims this law of grace, and every holy life in turn repeats it; the prayer of yes must be a momentary consciousness of being at God's disposal, of surrendering to His immense initiative.

This is fundamentally the teaching received and handed on by seventeenth-century authors when they spoke of "prayer of the heart" or "affective prayer," opposing it to the prayer of the mind or reflection; they even called it "prayer of abandonment," contrasting it with all forms of effort or technique.

The definition given by a great Carthusian Master-General, Dom le Masson, was this: "I call the prayer of

[112]Charles Péguy, *Eve*.
[113]2 Cor. 4:6.

abandonment this: that which is made without too much philosophizing about His name and His qualities, since it is enough to know that all comes from God and that all is to be attributed to Him; tends only to annihilate itself before God so as to be united with Him; is indifferent whether it be placed high or low in His presence, according to the place and position God wishes to give it; and desires nothing except the fulfillment of His holy love."[114]

Father Piny expresses it thus: "Prayer of the heart is nothing but a loving union of our will to the divine will of God. After having placed ourselves by an act of faith in the presence of the infinite majesty of God, we have only to remain in this union of heart and of will with God, affirming that we wish to be there so as to love God on our own behalf and, if possible, on behalf of all those who do not love Him; that we wish to spend this time of prayer only in loving, adoring, and recognizing Him for what He is, wanting to be there, praying and beseeching in charity for all who are to be loved in charity, desiring to remain abandoned to His divine will for

[114]Dom le Masson, *Introduction to the Inward and Perfect Life*, Vol. 2, ch. 6.

all He may ordain for us, and even more for all the crosses He may make us carry to give us reason to love Him with a most pure love. You must then suppress or put aside any secret desire to know or to feel whether you love, and be content with knowing that you wish to love."[115]

But to enter as perfectly as possible into Christ's "yea, Father," and to avoid slipping into a useless passivity, Christian prayer must set itself in an attitude of faith and become a complete gift of self.

The words of the Master that followed on the trembling of His spirit formally invite us to enter with Him into the bosom of the Father and to sink ourselves into the mystery: "No one knoweth the Son, but the Father; neither doth any know the Father, but the Son and he to whom it shall please the Son to reveal Him."[116]

So we are brought face-to-face with the divine perfections that we know, and with those of which we have no idea and which are God's secret. Our cleaving to God must seek, not to narrow God into our vision, but to raise us up to Him.

[115]Fr. Piny, *The Prayer of the Heart*.
[116]Matt. 11:27.

His name of Father tells us not only that He is more Father than any other father can be, but that He is a better Father than all fathers and mothers in the world put together — "of whom all paternity in Heaven and earth is named,"[117] as St. Paul says. He is "Father of Jesus Christ," "His Father." The divine paternity not only is the tenderest and the most affective toward us, but it also begets the Son, who is "the brightness of His glory and the figure of His substance."[118]

This is our "yes, Father," the yes of children who receive the splendor given to the Son; we are children of God through His freely given generosity, as the Son is by His essence and by partaking of the divine nature.

This yes ought to echo the great prologue of the letter to the Ephesians. We must take part in the great and exacting plan of eternal love in order to enter into God's good pleasure. "Blessed be the God and Father of our Lord Jesus Christ, who hath blessed us with spiritual blessings in heavenly places, in Christ. As He chose us in Him before the foundation of the world, that we should be holy and unspotted in His sight in charity.

[117]Eph. 3:15.
[118]Heb. 1:3.

Who hath predestinated us unto the adoption of children through Jesus Christ unto Himself."[119]

To enter thus into Christ's yes, it is essential for us to submit ourselves, through faith, to the divine point of view, to trust in His love and His desire to draw us to Himself. The prayer of the heart could never be true if it lacked the "enlightened eyes" St. Paul speaks of, which can see the great perspectives of God's plan and our final union with Christ in His glory.[120]

❧

Give yourself completely to God

Second, to live the divine yes in ourselves, we must eliminate all artificiality of words or feelings and give ourselves totally to God. Man's freedom consists in the fact that he is master of his acts and that he can choose his motives and their fulfillment. He gives himself to God by returning this freedom, by placing himself entirely at the disposal of God's good pleasure and by cleaving to His entire will, both in time and in eternity. He shows a true will to love God as much as he wishes to

[119]Eph. 1:3-5.
[120]Cf. Eph. 1:18.

be loved, an explicit acceptance of all God's present wishes for us — whether revealed to us by our conscience, by Christ's representatives, or by inward or external happenings — and a ready acceptance of all that He may ask. Here lies the substance of this yes. In this way, we need fear neither vain agitation, since all is contained in the simple unit of love, nor complacent laziness, since there is the supreme activity of the total and effectual giving of self to God.

The Liturgy asks for this disposition in one of its prayers: "Grant that your servants may love You with all their power and may accomplish what pleases You with all their love." Such self-giving in prayer includes and surpasses the zeal of the will to put ourselves at God's service, which St. Thomas sees as the essential act of virtue in religion. The act is prompted by the perfections of God, to whom man is thus eager to give himself, but it is, as it were, stimulated by the sense of our wretchedness; in this giving, man wants to put himself at God's disposal for His glory, and to escape from the misery of his sin.[121]

And this yes goes still farther and becomes increasingly simpler, because it is a gesture of love that "gives

[121]Cf. *Summa Theologica*, II-II, Q. 82.

us immediately to God to cleave to Him in spiritual union."[122] Such a prayer is instantly wonderfully purifying, since it frees us from all self-concern, all preoccupation with impressions, progress, troubles, and weariness; it is occupied only with God and with receiving all from His hand. This makes it even simpler and within reach of everyone, since it requires neither reasoning, reflection, or study, and it is possible during periods of tiredness or inability, during temptations and distractions.

By His prayer in the garden of His agony, Christ wanted to show His people that this prayer of adherence and abandonment was even for those suffering the pangs of death, for those crushed by wretchedness and sin — of others as well as their own — for those who have no further hope on earth, for those who sweat with anguish, for those who feel nothing but loathing for what is good, for those who are bored and disgusted with everything, and for those who are in fear and affliction.

This prayer of abandonment is thus both the first principle and the peak of the spiritual life. It expresses the first acquiescence in Christ's grace and becomes, as it were, the fruits of all our strivings and the culmination

[122]Ibid., art. 2.

of our love. Our Lady's *fiat* was the answer to the love that was offered to her; it was the entry into mystery — the loftiest answer to the most unequaled love.

This is why St. Ignatius, after unfolding to his fellow soldier the meaning of life and a sense of his wretchedness, after he had led him to his Deliverer and placed the soldier in God's service, recited this prayer: "Accept, Lord, and receive all my liberty, my memory, my intelligence, and my will; all that I have and possess which You have given me; to Thee, Lord, I give it back. All is Thine. Dispose of it according to Thy entire will. Give me Thy love and Thy grace; it is enough for me."

Fr. de Foucauld's well-known act of abandonment says the same thing: "Father, I abandon myself to Thee, do with me what Thou wilt. Whatever Thou dost with me, I thank Thee. I am ready for all; I accept all, provided that Thy will be done in me, and in all Thy creatures. I desire nothing else, my God. I deliver my soul into Thy hands; I give it Thee, my God, with all the love of my heart, because I love Thee and because it is a need of love to give myself, to deliver myself into Your hands completely, with an infinite trust, for Thou art my Father."

Chapter Nine

⚜

Answer Christ's call
to watch with Him

"Watch with me."[123] The request the Master addressed to His disciples in the garden of the agony is one He unceasingly repeats to the faithful through the course of the centuries. One of the functions of a Christian life must be diligence in watching with the Lord. To think that life with God separates us from the world and its miseries is to forget this pressing invitation made by Him "who is in agony until the end of time."

What does it mean, then, to watch? In no other circumstance of His life did Jesus Christ want the company of His disciples as He wanted it in the hour of His agony.

[123]Cf. Mark 14:34.

To watch with Him is to stay near Him by entering into His soul; it is to enter into the same feelings and His most intimate thoughts.

⚘

Watch with Christ
by atoning for sin

To watch will be, first, a loving care to think of sin in the sight of God. Thus, sin will appear above all as a resistance to love. "They have forsaken me, the fountain of living water."[124] "Jerusalem, Jerusalem, thou that killest the prophets and stonest them that are sent unto thee, how often would I have gathered together thy children, as the hen doth gather her chickens under her wings, and thou wouldst not?"[125] "He came unto His own and His own received Him not."[126] Sin is the no that refuses love offering itself.

Similarly, faith discloses the misfortune of the man who has lost God. "For what doth it profit a man if he gain the whole world and suffer the loss of his own soul?

---

[124]Jer. 2:13.
[125]Matt. 23:37.
[126]John 1:11.

Or what exchange shall a man give for his soul?"[127] "For if in the green wood they do these things, what shall be done in the dry?"[128] "Be mindful . . . that you were at that time without Christ, being aliens from the conversation of Israel and strangers to the testament, having no hope of the promise and without God in this world."[129]

From this, from the will to abolish such an evil in communion with Christ, an effectual desire will be born in the soul to love, to make up somehow for those who do not love, and to draw down God's mercy on the misery of the world. This will be the dominant note in a watching of atonement, lit by Christ's soul and desiring to labor with Him and remove sin.

With this as a guide, a man will run no risk of taking one of the wrong turns that too often spoil prayers of reparation: pride and sentimentality.

How many times do we think with the Pharisee, "I am not as other men"[130] or "We at least are pure and

---

[127]Matt. 16:26.
[128]Luke 23:31.
[129]Eph. 2:12.
[130]Luke 18:11.

faithful." We wish to make reparation, not because we think ourselves better than others, but because, as Christians, having experienced mercy, we know that it is not exhausted and that it asks only to be extended to all others, to all who are our brethren in misery. And even more because we know how our sins of omission, the inadequacy of our testimony, and the mediocrity of our way of life are the cause of our brethren's sins, we want to make reparation and pray for them.

This sense of having received mercy, which induces in a Christian a perpetual and humble state of thanksgiving, becomes one of the reasons for his trust. Behavior that abuses sinners is closer to pharisaism than to charity, which makes a man desire to excuse his brother. "Father, forgive them, for they know not what they do."[131]

Sentimentality can be another stumbling block. God was made flesh to speak to our senses, and His agony is infinitely pitiful; He made Himself unrecognizable; He appeared as a worm, as the lowest of men. But it must not be forgotten that after His Resurrection, He entered into His glory, and suffering cannot touch Him in any manner whatever; His kingdom is without end. Evil can

[131] Luke 23:34.

achieve nothing against Him, and the great visions of the final victory described in the book of Revelation must illuminate our progress in faith. Phrases such as "to console Christ," or "Jesus is in agony until the end of the world" and the like, although some have great value, must not cause us to stray into a path of affective melancholy or morbid piety.

Our Lord, who no longer suffers, desires that sin should be felt today by the members of His Body. It is all to the good if our feelings enter into this sharing in the divine reparation; but a true attitude of faith will always prevent us from falling into excess. Christ is the immortal Lord of the ages. Reparation should not merely resemble the consolations offered to a human being, even though such consolations enter into the divine reparation in part, since He wishes to associate His people with it.

❧

Remember that Christ is your reparation

To watch with Christ is, above all, to understand that He alone is our reparation. What can man do when confronted with infinite evil? Jesus gave Himself to us, and He remains a gift placed at our disposal for the Father's glory. His yea finally covers all the nos of the earth; the richness of His holiness is greater than the wretchedness of all sin. It would be presumptuous to think ourselves capable of making reparation or of saving; Christ alone can do it, and He gave Himself to us for that purpose. Adoration for the sake of reparation seeks possession of Him in order to be able to offer Him to the Father.

"What reparation can You still expect? Jesus, Your Son, has already paid in full." "We have an advocate with the Father, Jesus Christ the Just. And He is the propitiation for our sins; and not for ours only, but also for those of the whole world."[132] This inspiration, if genuine, will not be limited only to the time of prayer, but will transform the whole course of life, introducing a positive and vigorous force into it. A breach in a building cannot be repaired with fine words; it needs toil and exertion until it is repaired. This concern with reparation can become one of the most powerful spurs to give glory to God and to sanctify ourselves in order to make reparation for our brethren.

Such a spirit will create a joyful patience through all the tribulations we meet in daily life, so that they all

[132] 1 John 2:1- 2.

become means of union with the one great offering, that of the Lord Jesus.

But let us make no mistake. In starting from faith and placing ourselves at the center of the mystery of love, we run no risk either of removing ourselves from the actual state of the world in which we live or of judging it. On the contrary, we learn to love it and wish for its good, as God does. Much more important, we run no risk of becoming narrower, since, on the contrary, we shall discover a more lively sense of our wretchedness, our omissions, and the ties that bind us to our brothers. We do not run the risk of becoming hardened to the evil in the world, and its injustices and blemishes, for we feel them as harming God.

The prayer of reparation becomes the natural refuge for a Christian wherein he enters in order to exist with Christ and kneels to adore and to pray; he feels within him all his brethren who do not adore and as yet do not pray. He is responsible for them; he represents them; and charity takes on the vigor and the dimensions called for by its function as a "royal priesthood."

Chapter Ten

ॐ

Learn how to ask God for your needs

Prayer clings to God for His own sake. It is a total offering of ourselves, but it is also a petition. It is no exaggeration to state that this is one of its essential functions. It has a part in the process of grace and salvation as important as that of study and genius in the process of ascertaining truth, and comparable in efficiency to that of labor and techniques in the exploitation of the forces of nature.

Just as the order of grace rises above these natural orders, so does prayer surpass all other forms of human effort. But who knows how to pray? Whose request for union with God is truly so strict that it partakes of the all-powerful efficacy of His love? St. James said this in the earliest period of Christianity, and the marvelous examples that he chooses from the Old Testament amplify a Christian's shame at the inadequacy of his efforts to meditate on the Gospels with complete loyalty.

In reading and meditating on Christ's words after the Last Supper, we realize that nothing can be intended except strict intimacy with God, the unquestioning confidence of a friend. "Whatsoever you shall ask the Father in my name, that will I do, that the Father may be glorified in the Son. If you shall ask me anything in my name, that will I do."[133] It is inconceivable except in the position where His exceeding love has placed us. "It would be useless for me to intervene," He seems to say, "since the Father Himself loves you."

It would be absurd to imagine this prayer bringing God down to our level; rather, it raises us to God so that we can cooperate in His plans. The boatman who casts anchor does not draw the shore to his vessel; he approaches the land and settles alongside it.

⚜

Scripture calls you to pray for others
The place that the Gospel gives to the prayer of asking is enough to indicate its importance. Together with

[133]John 14:13-14.

brotherly love, it forms the subject touched on most often and at greatest length and it is summed up in the reproach that tells of the Master's disappointment: "Hitherto, you have not asked anything in my name," and in the words "Ask and you shall receive; that your joy may be full."[134] He promises the fullness of joy to make it clear that prayer takes us into intimacy with Him and gives Him to us.

Mention of the forgiveness we must accord to those who trespass against us to receive our own forgiveness from God explains how nearly our brother, even if guilty, touches God's heart, and how much the prayer that seems to "separate us from all things" actually unites us to all men. Being invested in Christ with a truly "royal priesthood," a Christian must understand that he is commanded to pray for his brethren; that it is both as one with them and also for them that he says we in his prayer. He has there a responsibility to exercise and a real duty to accomplish; to neglect them is desertion, leaving his post. He must pray importunately, like the Canaanite woman;[135] we might say with effrontery. He

[134]John 16:24.
[135]Cf. Mark 7:24-30.

must pray in order to know how to pray; pray both to obtain, and in thanksgiving after he has obtained.

⚹

Worship God through the prayer of asking

The prayer of asking is as much worship of God as that of praise. To beseech God is to acknowledge and proclaim His power and His mercy and that is why this prayer of asking must not be undervalued, although it seems to some people to be excessively human. The Lord said, "Call upon me in the days of trouble; I will deliver thee, and thou shalt glorify me."[136] This prayer of self-interest is often the means of arousing faith; it prevents a man from being shut in by the material world and relying on himself alone. To yield ourselves irrevocably is to believe in omnipotence, the watchfulness and the faithfulness of His love. "You will lack grace when my heart lacks power" was what St. Margaret Mary[137] learned from the divine Master.

---

[136]Ps. 49:15 (RSV = Ps. 50:15).

[137]St. Margaret Mary Alacoque (1647-1690), Visitation nun who received revelations of and promoted devotion to the Sacred Heart of Jesus.

98

Learn how to ask God for your needs

A sincere request is born of the consciousness of a lack in ourselves or in those we love, and it is addressed to someone who has the power to fulfill it. The Word indicates that we should put ourselves into a state of joy in order that our requests may be granted. "Delight in the Lord, and He will give thee the requests of thy heart."[138]

To ratify this teaching by His own example, Christ begins all His prayers with thanksgiving. He knows that He, who is the Son, has all His requests granted, but He desires to model the prayer of His people.

The Church's Liturgy has clung to this lesson, and it never addresses a request to God without recalling one of His perfections: "O omnipotent God, who hast made . . . holy Lord, almighty Father, eternal God . . ." and never ends without recalling the gift that incorporates all the others: "Through Jesus Christ, Thy Son, our Lord . . ."

By considering these facts, we can begin to understand the basis of prayer: all man's needs, all the world's wretchedness can become prayer; the creature's pleading becomes the expression of his love.

[138] Ps. 36:4 (RSV = Ps. 37:4).

❦

Ask God even for temporal things

But does not such a point of view exclude any purely human aspect? How can we ask physical and ephemeral favors of Him who promises great and eternal gifts? "Ask for great things, and small ones will be added to you," is Origen's conclusion. "Ask for heavenly things, and earthly ones will be given to you as well."[139]

We might be tempted, as was one of the people who spoke to Cassian, to regard prayer that begs for trifles as an insult addressed to Someone who promises infinite benefits. Why ask God for less than God, when God suffices? Ask for the countenance of God "that it may suffice you to ask only for what it will suffice you to receive."[140] Yet the very invitation to pray "that your flight be not in the winter or on the Sabbath"[141] would by itself show that God expects us to have recourse to Him in all our needs, even material ones; the daily bread we are to ask for only for today tells us to ask each

---

[139]*Of Prayer*.

[140]St. Augustine (354-430; Bishop of Hippo), *On Psalm 26*.

[141]Matt. 24:20.

day for whatever we need each day. Again with Origen we can enumerate the other requests the Gospels command us to make "for our persecutors,"[142] "that the Lord of the harvest ... send forth laborers into His harvest,"[143] "that ye enter not into temptation"[144]

The Father invites us to expand our wishes and our prayer. Man is inclined to cut short his prayer for fear of outwearing his credit — which shows that unconsciously he is relying more on himself than on God — but the divine teaching tells us to embrace the whole universe: God's glory, His kingdom, His will in time and in eternity, as well as all the needs of mankind. We can understand how such a way of praying removes egotism and nurtures charity. One of the great martyrs of the second century, John the Apostle's disciple St. Polycarp,[145] when he learned that the people had demanded his death with a great clamor and knew what was going to happen, withdrew to a nearby country house; there, following his usual custom, he prayed for the universal

[142] Matt. 5:44.

[143] Matt. 9:38.

[144] Matt. 26:41.

[145] St. Polycarp (d. c. 156), Bishop of Smyrna and martyr.

Church. Two days later, when the soldiers found him, he asked them for a delay of two hours, and during that time he prayed aloud for everyone he had known, both great and insignificant, and also for the whole Church. After that, he let them lead him to the stake.

This attitude, which draws the material for prayer from the world and the Church's needs, is no longer simply an expression of man's desires; it has become an expression of God's desires in man's heart. It is the prayer of fire referred to by Cassian and by St. Paul when he wrote of the unspeakable groanings that the Spirit shapes in the hearts of saints.[146]

This mysterious prayer in which God seems to beseech God through the human heart explains certain curious features in the lives of the saints, certain familiarities or excesses in their prayers for stubborn and despaired-of sinners. It also explains the "weaknesses of the divine friendship" mentioned by Bossuet when he talked about some of the saints' lives, for, if this ever-closer conformity with the divine will is revealed in what is desired and asked for, it is felt even more in the manner of asking.

[146]Rom. 8:26.

Learn how to ask God for your needs

⚜

Ask sincerely for what you need and desire

The spirit in which the prayer of asking should be made is primarily truth or sincerity. We must never ask for anything without really wanting it and being ready to work to obtain it. To ask for the kingdom of God without being determined to spend ourselves to get it would be an empty prayer; the cry of the voice would not hide the emptiness of the heart. St. Thomas More,[147] who prayed with sincerity, expressed it: "Lord, give me the grace to work to bring about the things that I pray for."

This truth implies also humility, trust, and perseverance. It implies humility, because it is impossible for anyone who genuinely thinks about it not to feel the infinite distance that separates him from the good things he asks for; it is impossible for him not to feel that by himself he is more than unworthy. "O God, be merciful to me a sinner."[148] It implies trust — infinite trust — born of the divine generosity: "He that spared not even His own Son, but delivered Him up for us all, how hath

---

[147]St. Thomas More (1478-1535), Lord Chancellor of England and martyr.

[148]Luke 18:13.

He not also, with Him, given us all things?"[149] And it implies perseverance, which will take the form of an importunity that will never desist until it has obtained, as long as it is the outcome of a real desire, not merely hot air and sentimentality.

⚜

Ask in Christ's name

The Master was careful to affirm these conditions; He both amplified and simplified them in words whose meaning we can never exhaust: "All that ye shall ask in my name . . ." And this is equally true whether the prayer be addressed to Him or to the Father.

"In His name" clearly refers to His mediation. The Father will refuse nothing that is thus asked of Him. But it would be sad to see in this mediation only an external or a mechanical action; it involves a transformation.

To pray in Christ's name is to allow Him to guide the prayer and assume responsibility for it; it is not to want this or that on our own account or by our own initiative, but to want it because of Him and for Him. The disciple's prayer becomes a human repetition of the divine

---

[149]Rom. 8:32.

prayer; it enters into His intentions and lets His Spirit pervade it. Because Christ has asked for it, and because He quickens it, it becomes His prayer in us, not only in what it asks for, but in its manner of asking. "Father . . . glorify Thy Son, that Thy Son may glorify Thee."[150] It aspires to what God wishes to accomplish and leans on what He has done. "Think upon Thy hand and upon Thy name . . ."[151] of Your deeds and Your sufferings, of the hand pierced for our sakes, the hand that was raised to bless us at the Ascension, and now above all when He is "living to make intercession for us."[152]

At these heights, the most burning prayer unites with complete abandonment, leaving everything in God's hands. "They have no wine."[153] "He whom Thou lovest is sick."[154] Why add anything? It is enough that Thou knowest, for Thy love does not fail. It does not sleep; nothing escapes its vigilance; and our most fervent desires are less than the gifts Thou art preparing.

[150]John 17:1.
[151]Bar. 3:5.
[152]Heb. 7:25.
[153]John 2:3.
[154]John 11:3.

"Father, into Thy hands I commend my spirit."[155]
This surrender remains the greatest even in the sinner
who confides himself to mercy and who, in so doing, is
united at one bound with the heart of God. The publi-
can asks for nothing but pity, and he comes away with
his prayer fulfilled.[156] The crucified thief asks only for
remembrance, and he receives a promise of being in Paradise with Christ that very day.[157] The *fiat* of immeasurable desire is identified with the *fiat* of abandonment,
open to receive all that God pleases to do or to give.
The *fiat* of the Annunciation answers God's hope and
contains the eager expectation of mankind as well as
God's gift.

☙

Ask in union with others

The prayer of asking has another path by which it
can reach this intimacy with God, a path so narrow that
in it the prayer becomes all-powerful. "If two of you shall
consent upon earth concerning anything whatsoever

[155]Luke 23:46.
[156]Cf. Luke 18:10-14.
[157]Cf. Luke 23:42-43.

they shall ask, it shall be done to them by my Father who is in Heaven."[158] This astounding promise ought not to mislead us. It ought to make us feel how great a detachment and how immeasurable a divine love are necessary to bring about this consent. Two can become one only by loving as Christ loved, to the point where God Himself enters that love. There is no risk that these two may unite in evil or shut themselves into egotism; by the very fact of their consent together, they will be open to everything and welcomed by everything. The divine promise offers us the treasure of a friendship that must bring about brotherhood that is universal.

In this light, it is easier to understand the power of the saints' intercession. We are aware of our needs, but we must also have the desire to approach the saints and to share in their holiness. This is especially true of turning toward our Lady, the model of the prayer of asking and of abandonment. For her, simply to say that there was no wine was to ask for a manifestation of divine glory; to desire that the divine word be accomplished in her was a communion in the most personal of God's plans.[159]

[158]Matt. 18:19.
[159]Cf. John 2:3; Luke 1:38.

Chapter Eleven

ॐ

Let your prayer
transform you in Christ

When we are honest in our relationship with God, prayer will ensure that we are true both in ourselves and in regard to the Lord's work and purposes. This is an essential consequence of our union with Christ, and it leads us to see that no genuine Christian virtue can exist unless it is born of prayer. Outside prayer there is only either the pharisaical virtue resulting from man's personal efforts, which culminates in a pride that sets itself up to judge others, or fine efforts that lack stability and constancy.

The moral effort that relies upon its own resolves counts on its own strength and fixes its own ideal, is bounded by a human circle, and it usually ends up in the attitude the Gospel so vigorously denounced in the Pharisees. Equally, spontaneity without effort and disguised as liberty cannot rise above the level of the senses and is all too liable to fade, since it relies entirely upon its own mediocre resources.

⚜

Grow in holiness through union with Christ in prayer

Union with Christ, of which prayer is one of the more conscious moments, produces a branch bearing fruits whose vigor and sweetness reveal the sap that has fed it. It is right to insist on the "without me you can do nothing"[160] that affirms man's inherent inability to do any supernatural work, but it is equally right to reflect on the "great fruits." Their abundance corresponds to the rise of the sap, and their quality must reflect the characteristics of their species. They are not human fruits, but the fruits of Christ; if a human life is able to bear any fruit, it is Christ's grace that has given the strength and inspired the ideal. The fruits are shaped by God's tastes and depend upon His grace.

[160]John 15:5.

Let your prayer transform you in Christ

Because of this indissoluble bond between prayer and life, all great spiritual writers have applied to this subject Christ's principle of discrimination: "By their fruits ye shall know them."[161] We must be in no hurry to judge. We must not be satisfied with the leaves, but must wait for the fruits; only through them will we be able to form an opinion. A life of prayer has, essentially, no other criterion of its sincerity than the transformation it brings to worldly life. Anyone who claims to be in contact with fire must show that his life is burned by it and that, little by little, he is taking on the properties of that fire.

This indissoluble bond, or, rather, this radical unity between Christian virtue and a living adherence to Christ is itself the nourishment of this virtue; it is not fidelity to an external code, but is a participation in Christ's grace.

This unity is affirmed from the very beginning of Christian life: "If anyone love me, he will keep my word."[162] It is the foundation of intimacy with God, for in such a man the Divine Persons will dwell. It will be

[161] Matt. 7:20.
[162] John 14:23.

consummated only in the glory where "we shall be like to Him, because we shall see Him as He is."[163] That is why St. John finishes by saying that he who is aware of such a destiny cannot treat lightly the requirements and conditions of such a life; he must aim at holiness. "And everyone that hath this hope in Him sanctifieth himself, as He also is holy."[164]

In this light we can understand the part that prayer plays in any life absorbed in being united to Christ. Even if it is a silent part, it is nonetheless effectual. It is impossible to love Christ and to rest in Him without becoming aware of His tastes and His ways of being and feeling.

"Impossible," St. Francis de Sales says, "to go into a perfumer's shop without becoming impregnated with his perfumes"; even more impossible to find our pleasure through love of Christ Jesus without becoming impregnated with His personality. This is why the transformation of life reveals the inward action of love; but this transforming love must be sought for, wanted, and deliberately pursued.

[163] 1 John 3:2.
[164] 1 John 3:3.

Let your prayer transform you in Christ

❧

Let's Christ's grace transform you

Anyone who thinks that prayer will destroy faults, correct bad tendencies, and make effort fruitful by procuring grace like a celestial rain is answered by "Man waters, but God creates the growth." Nothing is less external to man than God's help, as was shown by the allegory Christ chose. It is the sap that rises from the stock to the branches and makes them bear abundant fruit. Grace, and particularly permanent grace (*habitual grace* in technical language), which makes us pleasing to God, is always working in us toward union.

We must also remember that a prayer that asks for Christian virtues, especially those felt to be most needed, is likely to be granted unconditionally, since it is made so earnestly in the name of Christ that it runs no risk of refusal. If to gaze on Christ gives the desire and sets the ideal, if there is anguish at being below His standard and at failing to serve His ends, if there is a burning will to please Him and to follow Him, then it really is His asking in us, the expression of His desires, and the unspeakable groanings of the Spirit that beseech for the saints.

If prayer has these qualities, reborn again and again from the same awareness, if it beseeches unceasingly because it is part of the effort to lay hold of Christ as He has laid hold of us, how can it fail to have persever-ance that nothing can weary, an importunity that noth-ing can deter, and a humility that astounds anyone who sees it?

⚘

Offer God your free assent

"You ask and receive not, because you ask amiss."[165] Yet prayer does not owe its transforming virtue solely to the imploring power of its utterance. God deals in a wonderful way with His children. Bossuet used a good phrase when he spoke of the "profound respect" with which God treats human freedom, and it is not an exaggeration.

Because God loves man and has made him free, He will work nothing in him without his assent. Even if no active effort is needed, at least there must be consent and surrender on man's part. At the Annunciation, the archangel explained to our Lady what was to happen, and that her virginity was to become fertile; when the Lord chose Saul as His instrument of salvation for the

---

[165]James 4:3.

Gentiles, He warned him it would be hard to kick against the goad.[166]

But in most cases, God wants man to give himself freely and in this, as in all forms of education, to make a personal discovery of the ideal and its application, so that his way of thinking alters little by little.

It is interesting that modern psychological discoveries about the importance of the subconscious and what impregnates it, about the uselessness and the contrary effect of resolutions if they remain external and resemble constraint, and about unconscious deterioration merely confirm what has always been said about the effect of real prayer. Of course, we cannot reduce prayer to some human system of morals, or to a psychological analysis of the self and its tendencies, or to an artificial compound of attitudes and a kind of inner enthusiasm. On the contrary, prayer is both great and beautiful. In it the disciple listens to his Master, trying to absorb His teaching on a given point, to understand His ideal and the demands of His love; and the disciple is ready if necessary to abandon his own methods and to lose his own way of thinking.

[166] Acts 9:5.

The Little Manual of Perfect Prayer

There is the kind of prayer in which a man who sees that he cannot rise immediately to the heights waits for the "eagle's wings" that will grow from his hope in God, who alone is able to grant what he desires. There is the prayer in which the love of the disciple, learning the tastes of his divine Friend, is overwhelmed by the wish to please Him and to try to do for Him what He has done for us.

Meditation that remains a kind of cautious scrutiny, a mere reflection on the subject of virtues, hardly more than an exercise in the virtue of prudence, is in danger of becoming sterile and of deforming man by shutting him within his humanity and confining his efforts to that level.

In contrast, the prayer that seeks Christ according to His ideal and finds its delight in Him opens the soul to God; man is saturated by grace, and it changes his mind and senses little by little, bringing him closer to intimacy with Christ. True prayer, and the effects it produces, will not only bear the stamp of duty fulfilled, but will have the beauty of a love that is eager to please God.

These virtues will not be a transposition of the ego, to borrow psychologists' jargon; they will not be a disguised egotism or virtues full of bitterness, of unadmitted regrets and judgment of others; they will not be human, shop-window virtues that neither honor nor reveal God; they will be living, heart-felt virtues that please men (unless they detest them), because they correspond to what is best in man, and that pave the way to the presence of God, because they have a relationship with Him.

The best way to refute the errors of contemporary psychologists is to accept the truths contained in their reproaches, while realizing and pointing out to them that what they take exception to are distortions that we hate even more than they do, since we are concerned not with ourselves, but with the Gospel. Virtue born of a dialogue with God, a vocation nourished in such a climate, can never become a mere impotent refusal to face life, a negative attitude; it is a yes to the most beautiful of loves and is infinitely positive.

❦

Work to overcome your faults

It must not be concluded from these principles that prayer in Christian life ought to be restricted to the function of nourishing virtue. Perhaps in some phases of life this must be the case, but to stop at this point would be to forget the infinite richness of God's friendship. At some of the more difficult corners, it is necessary to halt and wait for God's direction; in stormy periods, we have to cling on like a limpet; but even when confronted by fundamental obstacles that obstruct the path, we cannot leave it.

A Christian threatened by depression must dwell upon his reasons for rejoicing, so that Christ will find him ready to receive the joy He wishes to give. A disheartened man must do the same until he has achieved hope. An irascible man, unable to bear the slightest irritation, must return untiringly to his gentle and humble Master; he must study His deeds and follow Him step by step in his working life, discredited, misunderstood, contradicted, and slandered; he must contemplate Him, as the Lamb who did not complain, until he feels himself curbed by the yoke that is easy and bearing the burden that is light.[167] The egotist must concentrate on the teachings about brotherly love until they are stamped on every recess of his mind and conscience. The proud man, full of presumption and self-importance, must find pleasure in his absolute dependence on the Father's freely given love, must rejoice in having nothing and in not

[167]Cf. Matt. 11:30.

being able to acquire anything except by accepting it from God. The man full of spite must adore God's freedom to give as He wishes, thank Him for what he himself possesses, for what others possess, and for what he has not received, until he has drained his secret abscess. Then in considering himself and others, he will have regard for God's glory alone and will feel that he is only one of the many members of the Mystical Body of Jesus Christ. The indifferent man must rouse himself and be re-forged in the fire of Pentecost. And a Christian afflicted with any of these basic faults cannot honestly approach Christ in prayer without admitting to it and without making an iron resolution to tear himself away from his fault, regardless of the cost, for Christ's love.

To pretend to pray without acknowledging an effect in our life is to introduce into the spiritual life an illusion and a disunity that will destroy it. It is to make advances toward the divine union and at the same time to flee from it. Life must rise to the level of prayer and start to become an act of charity, or prayer will become an artificial exercise whose laws and spirit are dictated by the ego.

It is not a question of tendencies that are recognized as unwanted and consequently combated, but of those accepted more or less consciously, and which, as a matter not of scruple but of fact, alter our whole behavior so much that they form a barrier against divine grace.

If we wanted to try to express more precisely the effect prayer ought to have on Christian virtue, we could sum up its influence thus: it gives virtue a motive and an inspiration; it strives to recognize its possessions, but from Christ's point of view, considering what it can give Him and what it can receive from Him, and how much of its vitality it can pass on. Prayer tries to share in His spirit, attending to His words and entering into His soul to find out how to please Him. Such thoughts, constantly reconsidered, will end by penetrating the depths of the soul and transforming the basis whence our most spontaneous reactions are born, rooting our actions in Christ Himself, bringing the branch more closely under the influence of its stock.

At a more advanced level, prayer should show us the ideal of Christian virtue, not as a mere abstraction or external code, but as a reflection of the divine countenance. It is a step, or rather a progress, on the road that is Christ. It is a characteristic of His soul and a communion with His life. It is Christ whom we must try to reproduce by careful imitation; we must be transformed into Christ by a spiritual *mimesis*[168] and become one spirit with Christ through clinging to Him.

Lastly, by making us aware of the distance that separates us from this ideal, prayer will help us conform more and more to God's will; and the more we dwell in Him, the more abundant will be the fruit we shall bear.

[168]Greek term signifying a more thorough imitation than is usually implied by the word. — TRANS.

Chapter Twelve

⚜

Listen to the Gospels

"Not on bread alone doth man live, but on every word that proceedeth from the mouth of God."[169] These words of the Son of God open great depths of joy for the attentive soul, because they promise that man can feed and live on God's penetrating light.

The Master, wanting His people to be holy — they are "to be in the world, but not of the world" in order to fulfill and follow their mission in it — offers us a way of life in which we can have complete confidence, since it promises us, in His name, the unfailing help of divine grace: "Sanctify them in truth. Thy word is truth."[170]

[169]Cf. Matt. 4:4.
[170]John 17:17.

Thus, we shall have the means of being preserved from evil and of becoming worthy of the mission that Christ has entrusted to us.

St. Paul says the same thing in another form when he extends these recommendations to all Scripture. He writes to Timothy, his friend and disciple who "was of the same mind,"[171] because he sought nothing except what is Jesus Christ's, "All Scripture, inspired of God, is profitable to teach, to reprove, to correct, to instruct in justice; that the man of God may be perfect, furnished to every good work"[172]

These suggestions, which refer only to the Gospels, are nonetheless true of all Scripture, for the Gospels are its synthesis and center, its soul and its culmination. "God, who, at sundry times and in diverse manners, spoke in times past to the fathers by the prophets, last of all, in these days, hath spoken to us by His Son, whom He hath appointed heir of all things, by whom also He made the world."[173] Although these words refer primarily to personal reading and meditation, they can equally

[171]Cf. Phil. 2:20.
[172]2 Tim. 3:16-17.
[173]Heb. 1:1-2.

be applied to the links that the Church's Liturgy and sermons establish between her children's souls and God's word.

We should never forget, even when we are alone, that this holy Book, this gift of God, has been preserved and handed down to us by the Church of the Apostles. To gain any benefit from reading the Gospels, it is important to have read and studied carefully a life of Jesus and some commentary on the Gospels; for however divine the Scripture may be, and however wonderfully universal its application, it is nonetheless true that it is a history of one country, one time, and one race. We would be greatly lacking in insight if we either ignored the historical circumstances of Christ's life or did not reflect on the exact meaning of His words.

For example, a knowledge of the Jewish background and the mentality of the Pharisees may be of particular value in the case of a certain parable or divine command; but to stop at that would be to give up right at the beginning; the shell must be cracked, as St. Jerome[174] said.

---

[174]St. Jerome (c. 342-420), Church Doctor who translated the Bible into Latin.

❧

Be mindful of the power
and beauty of Scripture

The Gospels are God's word, the teaching of the Word Incarnate; we must therefore reflect with wonder that these are "the words of eternal life,"[175] words whose beauty is at once ancient and ever new;[176] their transparent depth allows God to be seen, and they give strength and joy, fulfillment and life. They come from the very heart of Christ and are the expression of His love, for "the mouth speaks out of the abundance of the heart."[177] They bring us the light and wisdom that fill Him in whom "all the treasures of wisdom and knowledge are hidden,"[178] since He says that He has repeated to us "whatsoever I have heard of my Father."[179]

We must remember also the power these words possess, a truly creative power that transforms words into deeds. The Lord compares it to seed swollen with vital

[175]John 6:69 (RSV = John 6:68).

[176]Cf. St. Augustine, *Confessions*, Bk. 10, ch. 27.

[177]Cf. Matt. 15:18.

[178]Col. 2:3.

[179]John 15:15.

energy and giving promise of good fruits,[180] and St. Paul declared, "I am not ashamed of the gospel."[181]

In short, these words, the pre-eminent words, the only words worthy of the name (because they make a man live to the Eternal Word), express Him who revealed Himself as "full of grace and truth."[182] Nothing in the world can be compared with them, neither natural beauty, works of art, or the recollection of the heart or of faith, not even the relics of the true Cross. They surpass everything. Here, we should say with the wise man: "And I preferred her before kingdoms and thrones, and esteemed riches nothing in comparison of her. Neither did I compare unto her any precious stone; for all gold in comparison of her is as a little sand, and silver in respect or her shall be counted as clay. I loved her above health and beauty, and chose to have her instead of light: for her light cannot be put out. . . . For she is an infinite treasure to men, which they that use become the friends of God, being commended for the gift of discipline."[183]

[180]Luke 8:5.
[181]Rom. 1:16.
[182]John 1:14.
[183]Wisd. 7:8-10, 14.

Indeed those who use them become friends of the Lord, living in the confidence of His thoughts and of these words, which are the temporal and human expression of the Word of eternal God. These words are what St. Thomas Aquinas called the latter in the glory of the life of the Trinity: "Word, but not any word, but a breathing of love."

Of all God's gifts and tokens, only the Eucharist outrivals them. That is a more perfect expression of the Lord, for nothing shows so well as the Bread the extent of Christ's love and giving of Himself. The Eucharist brings not only grace, but the source of graces; and in it He who only speaks at other times is here really present in person, present in order that "as I live by the Father, so he that eateth me, the same also shall live by me."[184]

❧

Hear in Scripture God's
words spoken to you

Another characteristic to which we should be alive, if we are to improve our understanding of the Gospel, is the directness and vividness of each of the divine words.

---

[184]John 6:58 (RSV = John 6:57).

The Lord did not simply speak for all men or for certain privileged individuals. His divine knowledge enabled him to see and comprehend each one of us: "I am the Good Shepherd, and I know mine."[185] He spoke to each of us. Even when He was alone with the Samaritan woman and said to her, "If thou didst know the gift of God,"[186] He saw us all in His mind's eye and directed His words toward us to waken in us blessed yearning. When the crowd was thronging around Him to listen to His parables, the Master could see each one, and He explained to each in what mood He ought to receive the Word: "Behold the sower went forth to sow. . . ."[187]

In the same way, we ourselves are implicated in every scene of the Gospel, and we must react as if we were spectators or even actors in it. We have, we must have, some part with the leper who begs to be healed: "Lord, if Thou wilt, Thou canst make me clean!"[188] We must feel the depth of His friendship as much as those who saw Him weeping before the tomb of His friend: "Behold

[185]John 10:14.
[186]John 4:10.
[187]Matt. 13:3.
[188]Matt. 8:2.

how He loved him."[189] We must believe, with them, in the omnipotence of the love of Him who is the Resurrection and the Life.[190]

It is unnecessary to give more instances, but we must find this personal character of the Gospel if we are to profit fully from it.

⚘

Approach the Gospel
with reverence

In this light, we can understand with what respect and veneration, with what trust we ought to regard the holy Gospel. We can understand why the priest kisses the book at Mass after he has read the Gospel and why it is incensed as a symbol of adoration. Finally, we can understand more fully the liturgical prayers: "May the Lord be in my heart and on my lips." "Through the words of the Gospel may our sins be blotted out."

Once we have acquired this feeling for the Gospel, we must reflect what inward frame of mind will best dispose us to start reading it and to come to grips with it.

[189]John 11:36.
[190]John 11:25.

How should we approach it so as to be nourished by it? The question could be answered in one word: *love* — a love that listens must answer the love that speaks. The priest, carefully trained by the Church, kisses the words he has read. Trust great enough to abandon itself, love great enough to surrender!

Fr. Lacordaire says it admirably in spite of his rather old-fashioned phraseology: "What is there to say of the Gospel, since the Gospel is written? Open it, you that it has made my son, and after impressing your lips on it, give yourself to it as to the soul of your mother. She loved you, and she came from God. The Gospel also comes from God, and it is the only book that has received the gift of loving."

St. Paul speaks of "the fullness of faith,"[191] which fills the soul with joy, light, and peace, and binds it in unity with Christ. But the formation of this bond demands faith that can rise above the senses to share in the words and thoughts of God. It must be firmer than Heaven and earth; they are fated to "pass away," whereas the Master's words will not pass away.[192]

[191] Heb. 10:22.
[192] Luke 21:33.

This absolute faith that clings to God's word is of first importance, and we must strive to make it correspond to God's truth. It must be as perfect and as final as God is truthful. As for obscure and difficult passages (either in themselves or because they appear so to us), we must have humble recourse to prayer; we must give the matter our whole attention and refer to the authorized commentaries that will tell us the mind of the Church or at least the mind of an author whose knowledge can help us.

It is here we must have the humble and trusting attitude of Mary, who sat at the Lord's feet and heard His word.[193] The disciple opens his mind to Christ to allow himself to be molded by Him and to receive his Master's thoughts and soul in his own: "Teach me to see what Thou seest, to think as Thou thinkest, so as to live with Thy life."

We must also undergo what the Holy Spirit calls "famine," for there were days when God sent on earth a famine: "not a famine of bread, nor a thirst of water, but of hearing the word of the Lord."[194] Our attitude must be

[193]Luke 10:39.
[194]Amos 8:11.

that of a beggar with the eagerness of hunger: "He hath filled the hungry with good things," as our Lady said.[195] Hunger is the consciousness of a need, the cry of want. Thus, we are told to "take the book and eat it up."[196]

Further, we must become as little ones if we are to attain to Wisdom;[197] we must be as little children if we are to enter into the kingdom of Heaven.[198]

Finally, we must bring to this union a pliable soul, ready to receive the divine stamp and to keep it for eternity. The Gospel is the light of life. It is not something merely to occupy our intellect, but a seed that must sprout in our lives to make them similar to the life of our Master. Our docility must permeate our whole soul, making it entirely available to Christ's will.

All this brings us back to where we started: meditation on the Gospels must be a meeting with Christ, a communion in which He is received under the appearance of words and in which we are surrendered to His Spirit to be fashioned and moved by Him.

[195]Luke 1:53.
[196]Cf. Apoc. 10:9 (RSV = Rev. 10:9).
[197]Cf. Prov. 9:4.
[198]Matt. 18:3.

A Christian recognizes the voice of the Lord, and so he must, from the first, cry out with the young Samuel: "Speak, Lord, for thy servant heareth."[199] And he must remain thus, listening to his Master.

We ought not to be able to open the Gospel or to read or hear a quotation from it without instantly feeling a response in heart and mind that tells us we are in contact with what is dearest and most precious to us, what is holiest, truest, most beautiful, most decisive, and most passionately interesting in our life. It is the word of eternal life.

Hearing itself summoned by name, and recognizing the wonderfully personal tone that addresses it, the soul cries out as Mary Magdalene did when she was near the tomb of the Resurrection, not so much by words as by an exclamation of trust and love: "Rabbi, Master!"[200] Then a song of thanksgiving will arise in such a soul, for it can experience the full extent of its happiness proclaimed by the Master: "Blessed are the eyes that see the things which you see. For I say to you that many prophets and kings have desired to see the things that you see and

[199] 1 Kings 3:10 (RSV = 1 Sam. 3:10).
[200] John 20:16.

have not seen them; and to hear the things that you hear and have not heard them."[201]

We can say that when we start to learn a language, we have to be taught both the language and how to learn it. We could not understand Greek without knowing the language, and without a corresponding state of the heart, we cannot understand the language of love. We must exist in the Holy Spirit and be saturated with His unction if we are to have access to what He has said to us: "He that is of God heareth the words of God"[202]

It was this inner meaning of the Scriptures that Christ revealed to His Apostles at Easter, and we must constantly ask for this grace; we must knock at the door until it is opened, remembering always that this grace is the free gift of Christ revealing Himself to His people, because they live as He does.

❧

Let the word of God dwell in you

But a passing contact such as this is not enough; the soul must become a soul fashioned by the Gospel, a soul

[201]Luke 10:23-24.
[202]John 8:47.

fed on light, as chlorophyll is fed by the sun, so that, when the moment comes, it will be able to give itself back to God with the Gospel engraved on it.

Surely this is the meaning of the Lord's words: "If my words abide in you, you shall ask whatever you will, and it shall be done unto you."[203] It is not enough to have faint recollections after an hour's reading. It is also the meaning of the apostle's wish: "Let the word of Christ dwell in you abundantly: in all wisdom, teaching and admonishing one another in psalms, hymns, and spiritual canticles, singing in grace in your hearts to God. All whatsoever you do in word or in work, do all in the name of the Lord Jesus Christ, giving thanks to God and the Father by Him."[204] Here again the reference is to a permanent establishment, an abundance. The psalmist also said of God: "Thy words have I hidden in my heart, that I may not fail against Thee."[205]

Presently we shall discuss the gifts awarded to the soul in which the divine word lives and reigns; but let us first look at the means. Primarily there is the grace "coming

[203] John 15:7.
[204] Col. 3:16-17.
[205] Ps. 118:11 (RSV = Ps. 119:11).

down from the Father of lights."[206] It is so glorious for God and so precious for the soul that it would be impossible to devote too much ardor, humility, or trust to begging for it and imploring it. "Give us this day our daily bread," Thou who knowest the bread by which we live.

Then there is the prayer that at first waits and later seeks. To start with, we must learn carefully and by heart the most decisive words of the Gospel; I say *decisive* for us, because they should illuminate and modify our lives. A Christian, like the priest mentioned by St. Jerome, ought "to make his heart a library of Christ," and every time he is questioned, he ought to be able to open his soul and read there the divine answer.

Just as he knows the Our Father, a Christian ought to know by heart the Beatitudes,[207] the supreme words of the Sermon on the Mount, and the discourse and prayer after the Last Supper. He ought always to have in mind the divine commands and promises which bind his life, and he will soon acquire a great treasure if, every morning, he makes the necessary effort to learn one or two verses of the New Testament.

[206]James 1:17.
[207]Matt. 5:3-12.

But this is only a start; we must keep this word of the Master in our hearts, as our Lady did;[208] we must turn to it throughout the day as the subject of conversation with the Lord. Reflection of this kind will thus become more and more firmly rooted in the soul and will be enriched by daily experience. Daylight will remind us of Him who is light; the lilies and the birds will tell us of the protection of divine Providence; the ripening ears of corn will be like the harvest of souls ripened by grace; children will show us the ideal attitude; and further, the evils of violence will light up the blessedness of the meek, the cares of wealth will emphasize the blessedness of the poor, and the beauty of a peaceful soul will make us long for the Father. All things will unite in one voice, and this voice of creation will repeat the unique Word as if it were an echo sounding in our souls.

Finally, this way of thinking along the lines of the Gospel will grow from the habit of seeking the guidance of its light in all matters; it ought to be, in the beautiful words of the Old Testament, as the pupil of the eye[209] through which we see things and judge them, and by

[208]Luke 2:51.
[209]Cf. Prov. 7:2.

which we direct our steps. In every difficulty or doubt, the disciple will have recourse to divine guidance, knowing that his love cannot be better expressed than by fidelity to the divine word.

And thus, carried away by the Lord's Spirit, we shall go from glory to glory according to His ideal.[210] The Gospel will become a true friend, the conscience that speaks when our own is silent. Such a life, such an assiduous effort to follow Christ's Word, is logically the best means of preparing ourselves to understand the sacred text and the depth of the Master's thought. This cannot be said too often. "Everyone that is of the truth heareth my voice,"[211] and "he that doeth truth cometh to the light."[212] In the Old Testament, the Holy Spirit had already compared the eagerness of truth to go to those who are faithful and the irresistible instinct that makes birds fly together: "Birds resort unto their like: so truth will return to them that practice her."[213] There is nothing surprising in this, since Christ's words to His disciples

[210]Cf. 2 Cor. 3:18.

[211]John 18:37.

[212]John 3:21.

[213]Ecclus. 27:10 (RSV = Sir. 27:9).

were spoken in the mystery of a common life. The Master Himself asserted it: "You see me because I live, and you shall live."[214]

Two essential points must be made here. First, it is important to combine the meditation of the Gospel with the practice of the Liturgy. Every feast day ought to be an occasion for rereading and bearing in mind the Gospel texts relating to that feast. On the one hand, the Liturgy throws open perspectives and depths; on the other, it surrounds the Gospel with the grace of the Church's prayer. It reminds us of the special presence of the Spirit of truth which "will bring all things to your mind" as the Lord Jesus taught.[215]

Second, an excellent way of acquiring the Gospel point of view and the evangelical attitude toward life is to concentrate on finding out how the Master treated a particular subject, such as God's fatherhood, joy, the apostolic spirit, prayer, etc. Rereading and comparing all the passages relating to a special subject gives a deeper sense to the divine words and allows the reader to engrave each one on his soul, or even better, on his life.

[214]John 14:19.
[215]John 14:26.

❧

Be enriched by meditating on Scripture

It would be rash to try to enumerate the advantages of such meditation of the divine word. It is one of the favorite topics of both the Old and New Testaments. But briefly, it might be said that such meditation places the supernatural life against its proper background: "He who heareth my word and believeth Him that sent me hath life everlasting."[216] It means living the divine life to its full extent, a transformation in God, a repose in Him, and a life filled with His presence.

Our Lord, after the Last Supper, asked in precise terms for His people to be granted the holiness of truth: "Thy word is truth";[217] it was as if He wished to make us understand that there is no other atmosphere apart from the divine word in which holiness can thrive.

We can list other results, of course:

• *Stability and sureness.* Man is wavering and uncertain, unstable and changeable, restless as the waves and frail as foam. But if he will only build his judgment and his life on God's word, he will

[216]John 5:24.
[217]John 17:17.

be clothed in stability, unshakeable in the storm. This is the affirmation of the Divine Word Himself: "Everyone, therefore, that heareth these my words and doth them shall be likened to a wise man that built his house upon a rock. And the rain fell and the floods came and the winds blew, and they beat upon that house. And it fell not, for it was founded on a rock."[218]

• *Security*. St. Paul speaks of the "shield of faith"[219] against the Devil's attacks, and the Savior Himself taught us by His example that there was no weapon more effective against the adversary than God's word. To each of the tempter's attacks He replies simply, "It is written . . ."[220] "His truth shall compass thee with a shield," wrote the psalmist.[221]

• *Fruitfulness*. A fine tree with luxuriant foliage is welcome for its shade and fertile fruits at the

[218]Matt. 7:24-25.
[219]Eph. 6:16.
[220]Cf. Matt. 4:4, 7, 10.
[221]Ps. 90:5 (RSV = Ps. 91:4).

the Lord's law and murmurs His laws day and night"[222] prospers all his life. There is nothing surprising in it, despite the magnificence of the perspective. The being who has clothed himself in the thought and the wishes of the Lord enters into His omnipotence like a royal beggar. "If you abide in me and my words abide in you, you shall ask whatever you will, and it shall be done unto you."[223] Here, as always, the will to listen and the fidelity to put into practice in life are inseparably linked. A man who claims to listen, but who does not strive to live what he has heard is a liar; he deprives himself of all the benefits that the word brings.

• *Joy.* The psalmist was filled with joy as if he had seized a rich booty: "I will rejoice at Thy words as one that hath found great spoil"[224] — joy at knowing the truth and entering into God's secrets; joy in beautiful discoveries; joy from the highest and surest promises; joy from God and God's life.

[222]Cf. Ps. 1:2.
[223]John 15:7.
[224]Ps. 118:162 (RSV = Ps. 119:162).

"Blessed is the man whom Thou shalt instruct, O Lord, and shalt teach him out of Thy law."[225] It is the joy of Christ Himself that passes into us: "These things I have spoken to you, that my joy may be in you, and your joy may be filled."[226] He went so far as to compare it to the divine motherhood and said, "Blessed are they who hear the word of God and keep it."[227] Mary's soul, even more than her virginal body, was the pyx for the living Bread that had come down from Heaven.

• *The life of friendship with God*. Mutual trust and the sharing of plans and wishes are both the reality of friendship and its signs. "I have called you friends," said the Lord, "because all things, whatsoever I have heard of my Father, I have made known to you."[228] The wise man had said it many years before: "She is an infinite treasure to men, which they that use become the friends of God."[229]

[225]Ps. 93:12 (RSV = Ps. 94:12).
[226]John 15:11.
[227]Luke 11:28.
[228]John 15:15.
[229]Wisd. 7:14.

The unwearying meditation of the Divine Word gave all the holiness and joy to the life of the holiest of women, the woman who was blessed above all others. "His Mother kept all these words in her heart."[230] The Gospel says no more about the deep life of the Mother of God, for it is all contained in these words, and there is nothing to add.

We can guess, then, at the tenderness and urgency of the tones, and the imperious voice, full of promises, which, resounding in the soul of Augustine while he was still a sinner, turned his life upside down,[231] making him *Saint* Augustine, disciple of Christ and Doctor of the Church: "Take, read: the Master is there and he calls thee."

"Speak, Lord, for thy servant heareth."

---

[230]Luke 2:51.

[231]St. Augustine once overheard a child singing, "*Tolle, lege, tolle, lege* ['Take, read, take, read']." Understanding these to be God's words to him, Augustine opened the Bible, and his eyes immediately fell on the verse "Put ye on the Lord Jesus Christ, and make not provisions for the flesh in its concupiscences" (Rom. 13:14). Instantly, Augustine resolved to turn away from his sinful life and follow Christ.

Part Two

❧

The life of prayer

♣

Make your life
a continuous prayer

Prayer is good in all its forms, but, insofar as it is true prayer, it radiates and transforms the whole of life. The sap that the leaf offers to the action of the sunlight is going to give life to the whole tree; contact with light creates life in the plant, and the same thing happens with prayer.

In human activity, any element that is really alive tends to become a center of unification and of life. Prayer cannot seek to give glory to God without transforming the whole of life; it makes it a "royal priesthood" and a sacrifice of praise. Besides, without such unification, prayer would soon become little more than an exercise; there would be the danger of pharisaism at the center of the conscience, and life could easily slide into paganism.

The human estate does not permit even enclosed contemplatives more than a relatively short time for prayer. But even those for whom it can be only very brief are no less capable of the highest union of love with God. That is what is meant by "living our prayer" or "continuous prayer."

The Old Testament described it in an expression that is noteworthy because it was the basis of the covenant, and we know to what heroism of sacrifice, intimacy, and the collaboration in the divine plan that led the Patriarch: "Walk before me, and be perfect."[232] In Proverbs it is repeated as a promise: "In all thy ways, think on Him; and He will direct thy steps."[233]

The Lord made it a law telling people "always to pray and not to faint."[234] And He deigned to become Himself the model for such prayer, although by his very nature He is in God's bosom. He explains His life with God by saying, "He that hath sent me is with me, and

[232] Gen. 17:1.
[233] Prov. 3:6.
[234] Luke 18:1.

He hath not left me alone. For I do always the things that please Him."[235]

※

Answer God's invitation
to friendship with Him

Such a lifelong prayer conforms to God's purpose, for His love wants us to be with Him ceaselessly. But we must make clear what we mean by true prayer — namely, a permanent union with God, a worship that gives Him glory by praising Him, thanking Him, asking His forgiveness, and beseeching Him. It must be a life in communion with God, a life of perpetual prayer. Just as a nun prays in the choir and uses the means offered to her, so such prayer is made "through life," by means of life, making use of what we have to find God and be united to Him. Such a prayer is no sideline, but an inherent part of life.

The disconcerting words in which Wisdom, which seems to personify God, declares that He delights in being with the children of men[236] are less surprising than

[235]John 8:29.
[236]Prov. 8:31.

the truth. God desires to make man his friend, almost as if he could not do without man's comradeship. What is astonishing in the account in Genesis is the familiarity shown in God's walking in the garden: "They heard the voice of the Lord God walking in paradise at the afternoon air."[237] and in the call which is that of a man who wants to talk to his friend: "Where art thou?"[238]

The meaning of the Incarnation, which was designed to repair the breach in this relationship, is revealed to us by the prophetic name of the Son: Emmanuel, that is, "God with us." Indeed, all Christ's endeavors and His supreme Sacrifice are made so that "whether we watch or sleep, we may live together with Him."[239] Confronted with this great intention, surely we cannot fail to see how intensely God seeks us, to keep us with Him.

But this love that presses us cannot be satisfied in a few moments. "Christ died for all, that they also who live may not now live to themselves, but unto Him who died for them and rose again."[240] This needs no commentary,

[237]Gen. 3:8.
[238]Gen. 3:9.
[239]1 Thess. 5:10.
[240]2 Cor. 5:15.

but our love would be very weak if it did not concentrate ceaselessly on God.

※

Lead others to God
through your holy life

Finally, this "priestly" character obliges a Christian to turn to God in the name of his brethren and offer them to Him. It also obliges him to bring back to them, on God's behalf, the good things for lack of which they are dying. This responsibility has always been ours, but is more than ever necessary now, when intimacy with God is the only reply to contemporary atheism. Those who live with God must show the "godless" exactly who God is and with what life He can fill them: "These things I write to you that you may know that you have eternal life,"[241] and, it should be added, that all may know that you have received the life that is light and joy, justice and love.

But all words are inadequate; they have been too often misused; we must give visible proof of the truth. An object drawn upward demonstrates the force that lifts it,

[241] 1 John 5:13.

and a man who is sanctified through living with God demonstrates God's presence beyond all argument.

❧

Learn how to pray always

It cannot be said too often that such a life of prayer is far more important than any exercise in praying; moments devoted to prayer ought to pile up on one another until the whole of life is in fact prayer, which is why the great spiritual masters have always ranked the diffused prayer that consecrates the whole life to God far above any precise prayer limited to a fixed time. Fundamentally, of course, the two are inseparable; all true prayer tends to be unending; all life that turns toward God tends to create great moments when love can express itself fully.

Once we are convinced that prayer cannot be an artificial attitude, but must be true, it follows that to pray well we must pray always; that we either pray everywhere or else nowhere, either always or never.

Yet we would be wrong to imagine lifelong prayer as a protracted inward concentration with the same attentiveness and awareness as intensive prayer. St. Catherine of Siena characterizes continual prayer as the "prayer of holy desires" — a description it would be difficult to better. Desires can animate anything, and produce joy, pain, hope, or fear, according to the circumstances. They are not always explicit or conscious thoughts, but they are at the heart of all reactions. It is not possible for man on earth to keep the clear thought of God and His kingdom continually before his mind; but it is possible to love Him always, and to respond, at the level of deliberate reactions, simply by love. To make the whole of life a prayer is to react to everything with reference to God: by thanksgiving in joyful moments, by calling for help in difficulties (for others as for ourselves), and by praising God in any manifestation of His glory.

Because everything is connected with God's plan and His kingdom, everything naturally stimulates conversation with Him. It has often been observed that man is the priest of creation, because creation discovered the voice with which to hymn the Creator in man's intellect and heart; since creation is without a soul, she cannot do it by herself; with man to pray for her, she sings praise of God.

In the same way, the Christian must be a priest for humanity in general; this is the "royal priesthood" that consecrated him at his Baptism. Living among men, he must never cease telling them about his Father, and there is no circumstance that ought not in some way or other to become an offering to God.

This does not mean to say that such lifelong prayer can alter the nature of things and snatch them out of their profane circumstances — far from it. Things must remain what they are, and must become more and more real. Pity in trouble, simplicity in joy, conscientiousness in work: these things remain human, but the heart must be able to offer them to God. The miracle of Cana,[242] to take an example from the Gospels, was performed in order to manifest Christ's glory, but it did not spoil the feast; on the contrary, it heightened it by the abundance and quality of the wine.

Confusion about the true nature of things often causes misunderstandings that tend to oppose the way of thinking that leads to continual prayer. For instance, if compassion, instead of being a love very close to us that makes us share our brother's pain, becomes a pious, affected formality, it no longer shows Christ's charity; the same thing happens if joy lacks simplicity, or if work is without quality, and so on. The task is not to make

[242]John 2:1-11.

what is profane into something religious by words or by signs, but to link it with God so firmly that, through love, it becomes a work of holiness.

Lifelong prayer is a sharing in Providence's purpose, and it animates everything. Every person, every encounter, is a call from God; prayer opens the heart and answers, "Here I am," whether it is a question of receiving or giving. It does not matter whether it is a question of receiving from God some particular direction or of offering a particular attention to a brother, or a particular devotion to Christ's kingdom: these are sources of grace to anyone who lives in grace, which is what it means to live in prayer. "And we know that to them that love God all things work together unto good: to such as, according to His purpose, are called."[243] Prayer is the focal point for divine action that permeates the whole of life.

A faith reacting in love is the center of this prayer of holy desires. "Now that I believe in Him, all is crystal clear to me by His light."[244]

To achieve a life of prayer, the prayer must reach directly toward God; it must be rooted in God if it is to

[243]Rom. 8:28.
[244]Gheon.

dwell in Him, and the stronger the sense of God, the more it will inspire the remote and unexpected moments. Prayer must exemplify the vastness of God's love and be united to it if the whole of life is to respond to it.

But daily life must also include short and very intense spells of complete giving in prayer. This does not depend on time, but on an inward freedom that keeps us so closely related to God that charity can act in us. We might compare our attitude toward God to a radio station always ready to pick up broadcasting from a certain source but, by this very choice, closed to all other sources.

Prayer does not depend on time: "The work . . . is neither longer nor shorter than is an atom," says the author of *The Cloud of Unknowing*. And by *work* he means the perfect contemplative movement: "A blind stirring unto God." In this stirring, the soul must remain in an act of charity; thus it will "be in God, and God in it."[245]

---

[245] All the thought of this chapter is supported by St. Thomas's best doctrine. Questioning himself on the duration of prayer, he shows that the desire that is in the soul must always persist and that the duration or prayer properly so called must be measured in relation to the aims of charity (*Summa Theologica*, II-II, Q. 83, art. 13).

Chapter Fourteen

૪

Meet God in all that you do
and in all that you face each day

No element of the spiritual life, it seems, has been studied so carefully as prayer. Mystical authors have re-
peatedly analyzed its advantages and its needs. It has a
mysterious attraction for the faithful. This is under-
standable when we realize that prayer is the conversation between the loving soul and its God, by whom it
knows itself beloved, that it is like being "face-to-face
with the living God in the night of faith," and that it is as
necessary to the life of faith as breathing is to the body.
We would start on an endless path if we set out to quote
or to sum up all that the saints have said about prayer.
Guided by its light, the best authorities have recom-
mended long spells of its practice, and all contemplative

religious rules insist on at least one or two hours of prayer daily.

However, it is an indisputable fact that genuinely contemplative souls have often been deprived of their times of prayer; the lives of the saints offer many examples. And Christians living in the world and devoting themselves to Christ's service honestly cannot, whether they are priests or laymen, find time for long prayers. Does this mean they will be deprived of the joys, the strength, and the other benefits of prayer because of the circumstances ordained for them by Providence? Of course not. God's goodness guarantees this, and experience proves it daily. For those in the world, the answer is to make the whole of life a prayer, and to strive toward the highest union of love with the Lord, who is "the prayer of life."

We like to remember, when considering such souls, the holy priest who, when he found himself no longer able to achieve the prescribed hour of prayer because he was so busy, determined to do two hours; he took them from his sleep, a solution that is not open to everyone, especially in a world that sorely tries the nerves of its inhabitants every day. For them, the only solution is to make every day twenty-four hours of prayer.

Meet God in all that you do each day

Perhaps also it is not irrelevant here to mention that there are some temperaments that do not take kindly to long spells of prayer, even though they live by a faith that keeps God with them at all times, and are "moved by the Holy Spirit." Missionaries relate wonderful stories of such people, and there is no Christian who cannot recall some such case that has moved him deeply. Of course, discrimination is very necessary; not all simplicity is depth, but there are cases of souls of this kind that must be recognized as genuine by any spiritual adviser worthy of the name.

To all souls for whom long hours of prayer are impossible, a life of prayer is a necessity. It is not a matter of words, but of life or death; either they will reach the great life of love by this road, or else they will waste away into indifference; without oil, the lamp will burn out.

One last preliminary observation may be useful: classifications are always deceptive, particularly in a matter such as prayer, which unites the most vital and the most personal realities: God and the soul. It does appear, however, that some distinction can be made between the lifelong prayer that we are discussing and the habitual recollection pursued in the regular contemplative life. In each there is the preoccupation of a love that is aware that it has given nothing if it has not given all. It would be a terrible mistake to think we have given God His due by consecrating to Him one or two hours a day, and St. Francis de Sales stressed how preferable is prayer from the heart, spreading through all our actions, to narrow and almost mechanical prayer. But the professed contemplative will see in his habitual recollection — sustained, as it is, through all that he does — a continuous preparation for the exercise that will shortly call him to the choir. A Christian committed to the world, on the other hand, knows that his meeting with God will be made at almost any time, in spite of appearances to the contrary, in the middle of his so-called temporal occupations.

But it would be quite wrong to suppose these two types of prayer are opposed. Our Lord taught us differently, because, although the divine vision was eternally present to Him, He nevertheless spent long nights in prayer, and, in His agony, "prayed the longer."[246] To live prayer, we must pray always, but nobody will succeed in praying always unless at certain times he abandons everything else and is occupied in prayer alone.

[246]Luke 22:43.

༉

See the divine in all tasks and circumstances

The divine recommendation that enjoins ceaseless prayer is evidence enough that such prayer is our duty; but the Gospel develops this more fully. "Abide in me," the divine Master says again and again.[247] There is here no question of a disciple's entering into contact with the Lord from time to time, or of thinking of Him at more or less frequent moments. It is a question of establishment in Him, of an inclusion, a "reclusion" that allows nothing to escape. Any other attitude would be unworthy of God's hope and expectation.

And the first recorded words of Jesus — "Did you not know that I must be about my Father's business?" — are highlighted by the thirty years of life in Nazareth. "He went down with them and came to Nazareth."[248] This solemn announcement explains the mystery of those long and apparently insignificant years of His hidden life. "To be about His Father's business" is not only to preach, to pray, and to work miracles, but also to work at a humble job, rendering small services in an

[247]John 15:4.
[248]Luke 2:49, 51.

obscure village in circumstances without glory. And if we translate the text as "I must be at my Father's house," it comes to the same thing. From the moment the Child returned to Galilee, the Father's house is not only the Temple, but wherever His will leads His children.

From the time of the Incarnation, nothing is any longer profane; God reclaims the control of creation that had escaped from Him through man's sin. Human life, in its entirety, can be, and must be, divine. The Christian toils, and his work is the work his Master began; he renews his Master's actions; he eats at a table at which the Lord has sat and to which He has invited man. Man remains man, but he is part of God's family; he is only a branch, but he is quickened by the divine sap, and he bears fruits that are the Savior's. Earth is no longer a hostile place where an unhappy fugitive wanders after being cast out of Paradise; it has become once more "God's house" and the gateway to Heaven.

꒒

Remember the divine purpose of your life

From this point of view, we can really appreciate St. Catherine of Siena's proud answer to a soul complaining that it was hindered from perfection by its burden of temporal affairs: "It is you who make them temporal." For a Christian, everything should be divine and eternal. If it is not, it is because of his own faithlessness, because, if Christ has taken over the whole of life, then everything is an action of the Father, who numbers the hairs of our head. Constant and vigilant faithfulness will assure it. Unfulfilled resolutions and superficial offerings will not. A traveler does not need to remind himself of his goal at every step; all he has to do is to keep on walking in the right direction. But it is no good merely to say that he is on his way to his goal, or merely looking in its direction; he must actually walk. This is what we need to be most careful about, since the reality of the life of prayer depends on our constancy.

It is impossible to do Martha's work with Mary's spirit[249] (which could serve as the definition of life-long prayer) without total self-surrender. "All things are yours";[250] all is of use and will benefit you and lead to God, as long as you are Christ's. If you were not Christ's, nothing could be of any use to you. "To them that love God, all things work together unto good." Stop loving,

[249]Cf. Matt. 10:38-42.
[250]1 Cor. 3:22.

cease to be in love with God, and nothing is of the least use to you anymore.

We must therefore keep a careful watch on our motives to make sure they are more and more centered, and we must try to intensify them.

It is distressing that so many people are so engrossed by their material life, that they pass their time of prayer in thinking about all kinds of practical and material needs and in artificially dissecting their virtues and their sins, instead of simply looking toward the Divine Love, which ought to be the inspiration of all their actions.

The real essential is a moment's silence to place the soul face-to-face with the Lord, for whom, in whom, and by whom it must live. Prayer should replenish the well from which life springs. Prayer should say, "He loves me thus," and life should answer, "And I will love Him in the same way."

Many souls find the way hard, because they have lost the sense of the divine purpose in their lives. Materially, they "practice" charity and virtue, but they do not live in love. It is necessary to set up landmarks, beacons that can rekindle our fervor and the charity that must permeate our life. It must not be allowed to fade to a memory. Brief, spontaneous prayers and aspirations will serve excellently for this, so long as they are not mere formulas, but are soaring movements taking the soul back to God and entrusting it to the care of His Spirit.

⚹

Have the mind of Christ

The life of prayer presupposes a firm Christian outlook, what St. Paul called "the mind of Christ,"[251] and everything must be used to acquire it: reflection, study, meditation on the Gospel, sermons, advice, etc.

Awareness of the Incarnation, of the Word made flesh and of the Mystical Body, will establish in our hearts the earnest desire to continue Christ's work and consequently to imitate and reproduce it: to do what He would do as He would do it.

To achieve this, some people will keep one particular saying of their Master's in their minds throughout the day, treasuring it in their hearts, as our Lady did. Did not the Lord say, "If you abide in me and my words abide in you, you shall ask whatever you will, and it shall be done unto you"?[252] Eventually this will give us

[251] 1 Cor. 2:16.
[252] John 15:7.

the mentality of the Gospel, and we shall refer all our doubts and hesitations to its shining authority. Others will try to imitate their Master in their daily life; they will want to enter into the mind and heart of the Lord as He bent over the sick, smiled at children, and made sinners welcome. Their human joys will lead them to Cana, and their tears will fall on the stone of Lazarus's tomb.

Their sufferings are like bits of the Cross of Him who took on Himself all the pain of humanity, and they will become the mysterious "fulfillment" described by St. Paul. Their inward life is that new life which blazes in the risen Christ and blossoms like an eternal spring all around Him. In fact, Christ lives in them and makes all their life holy.

❧

Be at the disposal of the Holy Spirit
Another essential condition for lifelong prayer is to be completely at the disposal of the Holy Spirit. God is present everywhere, and His love allows nothing to escape; if we are to meet Him, we must respond to His presence. Too often we are so carried away by the bustle of our activity, so engrossed in our daily tasks, that no

real contact is possible. As St. Paul said to the Athenians, it cannot be difficult to reach God, "for in Him we live and move and are";[253] but we run away from ourselves and from Him.

※

Live in God's will

All these reflections lead to one conclusion, and it is the only one that matters: life becomes prayer if it is lived in God's will. But let there be no mistake; it is not a question of words, or of surface offerings; it must be a spirit, an attitude, an inward passion that makes us look for, and do, the will of our Father who is in Heaven, in all things. On more than one occasion, Jesus defined this union with God: "My Father . . . hath not left me alone. For I do always the things that please Him."[254]

At such a level, all is transformed; there is no success or failure, no joy, no pain, no obstacles, no plans, no rest, no labor, no dryness, no consolation, no self-seeking: nothing matters except what pleases God, what He sends, and what He asks. Nothing is closer to Heaven

[253] Acts 17:28.
[254] John 8:29.

than such a life; that is why Christ taught us to ask as the supreme favor: "Thy will be done on earth as it is in Heaven."[255]

The soul that has acquired this sense of the divine will is like a priest gathering the smallest fragments of the Host, with reverence not for what they appear to be, but for what they are: the Body of Christ. To such a soul, everything is prayer; everything is a means to union with God and communion with the loving presence of the Trinity. Activities, household duties, great responsibilities, sickness or health, silence or speech, prayer or recreation: all are meetings with God, opportunities to please Him, to cling to Him, and to grow in His love.

The whole of life has become prayer, a rising toward God, or rather, the possession of God and His embrace. Such a soul has found its Heaven on earth because it exists the whole time for God, in Him, and with Him.

❧

Find union with God through prayer
This form of prayer involving the whole of life in the complete fulfillment of what pleases God leads to the

[255]Matt. 6:10.

highest point of union. Christ promised it expressly: "He that hath my commandments and keepeth them; he it is that loveth me. And he that loveth me shall be loved of my Father; and I will love him and will manifest myself to him."[256] "If anyone love me, he will keep my word. And my Father will love him, and we will come to him and will make our abode with him."[257] Only a fool would disdain this humble life, which, without heroics or long spells of prayer, possesses God as a secret which lights from within.

This lifelong prayer will often be made in darkness and with great effort and toil; it will often be crucifying; but it also has joy and an abundance of the gifts of the Holy Spirit, even the most contemplative, such as wisdom and understanding. Their influence will be most noticeable in the firmness and sincerity of faith, in the desire for God, the sense of His love, in the ability to refer everything to Him, and in an understanding of His plans. A soul in this state appears indifferent to everything because it has risen above everything to God; but it is really intense and fervent in everything — in work

[256]John 14:21.
[257]John 14:23.

as well as prayer, in sickness with its idleness as much as in health with its labors. Indifference and intensity, detachment and possession of God, acceptance of everything and all men demonstrate its unity and harmony. If they do not, it is not truly lifelong prayer.

Often also a life of prayer will have genuine "experiences" of God — for instance, in a lightning answer to an impromptu prayer, the joy of a conversion, sudden participation in joy of Heaven, which our Lord described — and much more besides. God is not short of means, and He can create the most surprising opportunities to give Himself to the man who has given himself totally to Him.

❦

Rely on grace

But in spite of such assertions, it may be good to deal with a doubt that often arises. Is not such prayer reserved for a few privileged souls who can unite recollection with an active life, and can join the self-mastery that keeps itself detached from the world with the devotion of complete self-giving? Undoubtedly, such prayer reaches the highest level, but it is nevertheless meant for all.

Grace helps achieve it. Communion is intended to bring about precisely this result: "He dwelleth in me and I in him" — what is meant cannot be a momentary union. "As the living Father hath sent me and I live by the Father, so he that eateth me, the same also shall live by me."[258] The Resurrection, which we share by our Baptism, is meant for the sanctification of the whole world. Our sanctification will be fulfilled at the end of time by the resurrection of the body and the creation of a new earth and a new Heaven; in the meantime, it is carried out through the transformation of the Christian soul, and Christ's increasing influence over our smallest desires and our every action. This is the "abundant fruit" borne by those who dwell in Christ and achieve this life of prayer.

⁂

*Look for the eternal
significance of all that you do*

Yet, if there is the existence and action of grace, we on our side must provide a generous faith. That is our share, and we must face the fact that faith and generosity of

[258]John 6:58 (RSV = John 6:57).

the caliber required have nothing trivial about them. We must pray for them humbly and trustingly, and must constantly try to be worthy of them.

On this subject, Bl. Peter Julian Eymard[259] gives two pieces of advice that can form our conclusion. First, there must be a central thought that is both simple and effective and to which we can easily return: the idea of God as Father, of our Lady, of our most recent Communion, of the gifts of the Holy Spirit, or, more simply, of God's love for us. Second, we must find spiritual nourishment in what we do; all action has value, either in itself or in what it represents or recalls. We must look through each action of our life as if it were transparent, and we shall thus discover the wonderful pattern of the divine purpose, with its basic design of labor and rest, sorrow and joy.

To anyone who can see it thus, everything has an eternal significance and speaks of God, who desires to give Himself to us. In this light, everything is truly holy, and to live in this light is to live in prayer, in a secret conversation with our Father in Heaven.

---

[259]Bl. Peter Julian Eymard (1811-1868), writer and founder of the congregation of Priests of the Blessed Sacrament.

Meet God in all that you do each day

Possess your soul in God

To be able to give ourselves to this ideal, we must possess our soul. We can give only what we have, says the proverb. Now, possession of our soul cannot be achieved without the harmony of life that makes for balanced nerves, energies, and emotions. A hard life, a life of immolation, can still be a balanced life; but a life without human roots and without normal social ties, a life that is feverish and disordered can never be balanced. Heroism and dissipation of energy may sometimes look alike, but they are on opposite sides of the gulf between order and disorder, and God does not live in a whirlwind.

Man must possess his soul in God. Self-mastery and harmony of life are the preliminaries that will culminate in turning to God; and this demands constant practice of all virtues that can cleanse us and teach us detachment, and of the theological virtues that concern our closest relations with God.

This is the price of making the whole of our life prayer, and it is the beginning of eternal life. A Christian who has thus become a "living prayer" will be like the archangel sent on a mission to men, like the Word made flesh, sent into the world as his Lord was sent. "As Thou hast sent me into the world, I also have sent them into the world."[260] *As* means in the same spirit, for the same purpose, so that all may glorify the Father and return to Him. And it is thus easy to understand that this living prayer is the summit reached only by climbing all our life and giving ourselves completely to the task.

[260]John 17:18.

Chapter Fifteen

Accept God's will in all things

There is one aspect of lifelong prayer to which we must pay special attention, for it is essential: the fulfillment of the divine will. It would be interesting to take the teachings of Scripture and spiritual writers on this theme and to see how certain of the ancient philosophies, particularly that of the Stoics, sometimes came very close to it, and how the worship of duty in the Kantian or secularized conscience, is more or less inspired by it.

It is sufficient here to repeat the words Christ used when He deigned to explain for our instruction that although He is by His proper nature "in the bosom of the Father,"[261] His unceasing union with the Father was due

[261]John 1:18.

to His faithfulness in doing the divine will — words that we have already considered in another context: "He that sent me is with me, and he hath not left me alone. For I do always the things that please Him."[262]

※

See God's will in all circumstances

When He says, "Whosoever shall do the will of my Father that is in Heaven, he is my brother, and sister, and mother,"[263] we learn from His own lips that there is no intimacy so deep, so simple, and so full of tenderness and joy as that which is found in doing the will of the Father.

Here, then, is a sure way to life with God; it is guaranteed by God Himself and provides the most commonplace daily life with possibilities of the highest divine union that others are called to seek in particular forms. In the street or the factory, in the melee of the rush hour, we can have what is given to others in silence and solitude: "We will come to him and will make our abode with him." This is not to decry the means by which God

[262]John 8:29.
[263]Matt. 12:50.

calls certain people, but to show that the essential thing is common to all these means.

This sense of God's will is, therefore, of the greatest importance to all who seek to live with God, and it teaches laymen that they will lack nothing if they desire to enter into this mystery: "If God Himself were to give us masters," Pascal said, "how readily we should obey them! Necessity and events are just such infallible masters."[264] This reflects the most Christian and filial conformity to God's will.

Moreover, there is here a solution to one of the problems we mentioned earlier: modern man, child of "the second industrial revolution," is tempted to live with God less and less as he learns more and more of the laws of nature; he appears to control them better and to make better use of natural forces, because he knows them better and he applies them more strictly. The universe becomes to him more and more a question of formulas. How can he find the living God in a formula?

To recognize the Creator's will in the laws of science is a more certain guide to God than any childish idea of

---

[264]Blaise Pascal (1623-1662; philosopher and mathematician), *Le Mystère de Jésus*, ed. Brunschweig, no. 55.

coincidence or chance. Carrel's friends know how much he owed to the rigor of his scientific training and how, for him, it was the means of approach to the true life in spite of his own ignorance.

But the fact that this road is straight and open to everyone does not mean that it is easy in the ordinary sense of the word; it demands everything, since it is total and absolute; it is, as Piny says, "the means of means, the means without means. One can only find God in God and only when one has left all else for Him."

Everything, absolutely everything, depends on the divine will: "For of Him, and by Him, and in Him are all things,"[265] but He speaks in different ways to creatures who have no freedom and to those who are blessed with it; in different ways to those who stay in their own order and to those whom He has raised to His order, to that freedom which we call *charity*. Creatures without freedom are guided by the divine will according to their needs. Those who are free must comply with His will freely. That is why God speaks to their conscience by His commandments; He commands those who are united to Him by the grace of adoption through the action of

[265]Rom. 11:36.

His Spirit. To cling to God's will inevitably involves all this.

If we love God's will and want to do it, we love it and find it in everything. When we realize the scope and the depth of such adherence, we begin to appreciate St. Paul's prayer: "We . . . cease not to pray for you and to beg that you may be filled with the knowledge of His will, in all wisdom and spiritual understanding; that you may walk worthy of God, in all things pleasing, being fruitful in every good work and increasing in the knowledge of God, strengthened with all might, according to the power of His glory, in all patience and long suffering with joy."[266]

<hr />

Let your adherence to God's
will be universal and absolute

This opens up a whole train of thought: this adherence, to be genuine, must be both universal and absolute. Universal in that it must extend to the entire dominion of God's will both in the natural order and in human affairs, on the natural level as well as on the

[266]Col. 1:9-11.

supernatural. Even if the opportunity for our yes is a commonplace incident or an unimportant law, it has the value of an opening to infinity. Patience in illness, love of work well done, a professional conscience, and scientific objectivity can all become ways of sharing in God's will; and this beauty can light up both human wretchedness and human greatness, can transfigure both man's pain and his striving. Limitations and inabilities of all kinds can open the door to infinity. Such universality, if it is to be true, must embrace not only what we know, but also what we do not know.

The adherence to God must also be complete. It would be wrong to restrict it to what happens to us and to what we experience, for it demands also our own effort and struggle to accomplish His will. It is inherent in what is outside us and brought about without us, but nevertheless we must achieve it. The struggle against injustice, for instance, must be as intense as our patience in suffering injustice. It is because this positive and demanding aspect of God's will has been forgotten that Christianity is often represented only as passive resignation with nothing of its creative zeal. Love of God's will demands both acceptance of what happens and the effort to accomplish what is pleasing to Him.

That is why it must involve abandonment of everything to God's good pleasure and being at His disposal in whatever He may ask.

What has been said makes it clear that such loyalty to God is on a plane far above mere emotion, and suggests that docility to the Holy Spirit is what trains the human will and brings it into communion with God's will.

❧

Cling to God's will out of love

This summary of the inward dispositions needed to make such a conformity genuine leads us to another line of thought that also helps us see something of the riches hidden along the path of life with God. It is not a matter of mechanically performing what pleases God. It is not primarily our works that interest Him, but ourselves. He attaches more importance to the motive for our adherence to Him than to the adherence itself.

If we suffer the divine will without acquiescing in it, we are acting as machines, not free men, far less children of God. God looks at the human heart, at the person who has chosen to give himself. He desires the intention more than the action. Our adherence must therefore, if it is to be worthy of God, spring from love and exist to please Him.

To do our duty from pride, or to seek our own excellence in terms of human values or interior attitudes, will never lead us to God. Far from waiting on God, we are refusing to do so.

On the other hand, to do our duty conscientiously, simply because it is good, is a form of implicit love of God, which usually precedes an explicit love enlightened by the knowledge that God wishes to reconcile everything in Christ. This is one of the roads that leads to the conversion of many good pagans.

❦

Glorify God in all that you do

But a Christian who wants to live his Faith, and find a life of intimacy with God in adherence to the divine will, will not be content with an implicit love, but will seek one that is conscious, real, and deep. It is Christ who is this Christian's model in doing the will of God; it is Christ whose words reveal what pleases God: "My meat is to do the will of Him that sent me";[267] not

[267]John 4:34.

merely to suffer it, or to do it externally and precisely, but to live on it and to find in it joy and strength.

It is here that Christ's soul points the way to the heights; He says, in His prayer, "Father, glorify Thy Son," and again, "I have glorified Thee."[268] Perfect adherence to God's pleasure, or better, the communion that makes us one with Him, implies clinging to God's will in everything and in whatever way He wants it.

God is in everything except sin; all depends on His will, but He wants only to draw everything to Him by giving Himself and in order to give Himself: that is His glory. This is what it means, then, to will what God wills as He wills it, and to say with Christ, "Yes, Father, for it has been Thy good pleasure." At such a height, action and contemplation are identical; everything leads directly to God; there is no need to search for the route, because God Himself is there: "If anyone love me, he will keep my word. And my Father will love him, and we will come to him and will make our abode with him."[269]

This reminder of some essential principles is enough to indicate both the demands and the rewards of simply

[268]John 17:1, 4.
[269]John 14:23.

conforming to God's will; in the beginning, it seems a commonplace, hardly distinguishable from meticulous performance of duty, but, because God is love, this adherence lifts us to a life of closest intimacy with Him.

We can understand why St. Paul, considering the mystery of the Cross, seems to pick out the obedience of Christ and tell us that this obedience is the heart of everything and gives everything its value, and that fidelity in things that oppose our will and immolate it will lead us to the same peak.

It is difficult to abandon ourselves except by attaching ourselves to what will cost us something. This is the meaning of all crosses; they invite us to give ourselves to seek the divine will. But their value does not come from what they cost us, but from how much of it we are offering to God. All opportunities, all occurrences, and all obedience must become our ascent to the infinite, our encounter with love: "My Father will love him. . . ."

Jacob stopped at the roadside, and the stone he used for his pillow suddenly appeared to him as "the house of God, and the gate of Heaven,"[270] the foot of the ladder that joins earth to Heaven. Christ came to be "about

[270]Gen. 28:17.

His Father's business,"[271] to glorify Him, to establish His kingdom and reveal His name. And we see Him "going down to Nazareth,"[272] living the life of all young people, with years of submission and apprenticeship followed by obscure toiling, just like everyone else.

In descending thus, the Son of God has extended the privileges of the Temple to the entire human race; there is now no meeting, no stone, no situation that cannot be, for His people, their "Father's business." Even eating and drinking ought to be divine. It is not enough merely to speak; in teaching us to desire — and to desire it enough to ask God for it — that His will be done on earth as it is in Heaven, our Lord also taught us that we live, with Him, in God.

[271] Cf. Luke 2:49.
[272] Cf. Luke 2:51.

Chapter Sixteen

❧

See God in your neighbor

One of the most important aspects of our life with God is our fraternal life. The first Christians repeated to each other, as coming from the Master Himself, the wonderful words the Gospels have not preserved: "To see our brothers is to see God."[273] How can we fail to understand that our neighbor is given to us as a traveling companion, so that, through him, we may be on better terms with God?

A Christian can never repeat Seneca's phrase "Every time I have been with men, I have come back less man"

---

[273]St. Clement of Alexandria (c. 150-c. 215; theologian), *Stromata*, Bk. 1, ch. 19, and Bk. 2, ch. 15. Tertullian, *De Oratione*, 26.

without profoundly altering the sense. A Christian's contacts with men do not leave him disillusioned, scornful, and ready to think he belongs to a superior race; on the contrary, he feels himself to be more a part of them, nearer to them, more sensitive to their miseries, and more indebted to them. Not only, like St. Francis de Sales, does he want to be "man and nothing more," but he knows that thus he is made holy by closer union with Christ. Not only do men not separate the Christian from God, who gave him life, but he meets God in them, and his union with them brings him closer to God; to be with them is to be with God.

But some stipulations are necessary if we are not to distort this doctrine; its very loftiness exposes it to misapplication in the hands of those who lower it to their own level instead of accepting its demands and letting themselves be lifted to its heights. It would be a betrayal of the Gospel to suppose that every human encounter was this reunion "in His name," or to imagine that all human contacts are, of themselves, charity, and that all affection is part of the love with which Christ loves.

The very fact that Christ spoke of the heathen way of loving as insufficient, and that St. Paul wrote of distributing all one's goods to feed the poor and still lacking charity,[274] shows clearly that there is one way of loving and serving our brethren that unites us to God, but that there is, alas, another way which "profiteth me nothing" and is worthless.

There is a great danger of setting ourselves far below the level of the Gospel ideal, and then our relations with our neighbor will always lack the essential; they are not in communion with Christ.

Nor may we ever think of our neighbor as a means to our own perfection, or regard charity as a "means"; this would be complete distortion. The way in which some authors talk of our neighbor as a trial to be borne, of social life as a penance, of the service of our neighbor as a means of acquiring merit, and so on, is certainly not without truth; but it runs the risk of forgetting the important thing: we must love our neighbor as ourselves and therefore desire his good as much as our own; brotherly love is the essence of perfection and is not therefore just one means among many; the unity between Christians ought to be like that between Father, Son, and Holy Spirit.

[274] 1 Cor. 13:3.

Finally, it is not a question of condemning the hermit's vocation. It is noteworthy that the solitary and contemplative vocation has resulted in the formation of the closest communities — even though strict enclosure and impenetrable grilles may separate them from the rest of the world. But even the vocation to absolute solitude can never at any time form a barrier between the hermit and the rest of the Church; the hermit exists with his brethren and for his brethren; he lives the brotherly life intensely and supremely, and it is not this aspect with which we are here concerned. What we have to discover is how daily life and its contacts can and must become a union of love with God.

❦

Serve your neighbor out of love

There is a way of being with our neighbor, a way of loving and serving him, of bearing with him and understanding him that makes us one with Christ; there is a way of being with our neighbor that fulfills the Lord's greatest wish, and it is, indeed, the only way that embodies the ideal He has for His people. It is this ideal that is mysteriously to be realized in the Communion of Saints and the life of the Mystical Body, that we are to seek in the humble realities of daily life and the ordinary routine of daily contacts. This ideal, which shines in heroic acts, in sublime devotion and complete forgiveness, must illumine apostolic effort, shine in the life of the family and the neighborhood, in the commonest contacts as well as fleeting ones, in those we have to make just as much as in those we choose. A Christian must always love as Christ loves, and each human contact must be in charity so that God Himself will be present in it.

It is not the words we use (they may be as simple as the "Good morning" of our Lady at the Visitation) or the size of the service (a glass of cold water) or the pronouncing of the Lord's name (to judge by the astonishment of the good and wicked in the parable of the Last Judgment) that constitute the act of charity, but the inward spirit that prompts it. "You did it to me."[275] "With what measure you mete, it shall be measured to you again."[276]

This implies, for the disciple who learns from Christ how to love, the will to love in Christ's way. We cannot love as much, but He commands us to love "as He has

[275]Matt. 25:40.
[276]Matt. 7:2.

loved," in His way, by His light, and in His spirit. That means being aware of the bond that unites our neighbor to God, to the love that has adopted Him and waits for Him: "And the glory which Thou hast given to me, I have given to them, that they may be one as we also are one."[277] From this will be born the need, the desire to give our brother all that is good in our life, and to share our joy with him; we wish "that he may be in God," as St. Thomas expresses it,[278] even if this desire must remain a burning secret at the bottom of our hearts.

This way of living springs from faith and is born "of the water and the Spirit";[279] we should therefore often rise to these heights again by meditating on the Lord's words, by contemplating His plan for us, so that we will come to look at those who are united to us by blood, by society, or by profession with His eyes and in His light, and so that it will be through Him that we meet them. Otherwise our charity will grow lukewarm and routine.

We must turn to this thought again and again, so that it will pervade our actions, impregnate our feeling,

[277]John 17:22.
[278]*Summa Theologica*, II-II, Q. 25.
[279]Cf. John 3:5.

and increasingly renew unremittingly the heart that loves, understands, and serves in the way of Christ.

❧

Extend your love even to the unlovable

In this field, as in everything spiritual, there is a danger of illusion, and yet, to anyone who is attentive, there are many criteria that could almost be said to be infallible. There are numerous occasions on which no love except pure charity could survive. The great test of the supernatural reality of this way of loving is its universal nature, which makes no exceptions and can embrace all men, even those we do not know and those who have wronged us, who are against us, or who appear to be against God's kingdom. "You shall be sons of the Highest, for He is kind to the unthankful and to the evil."[280]

In the same way, the patience to endure and the generosity to forgive those who have offended us, as well as those who have disappointed us, who anger us, or have hurt us, can only spring from God. At any lower level, how could we have the feelings of God?

[280]Luke 6:35.

Such charity would have respect, time, and understanding for each of our neighbors, even if we have to oppose him and resist his egotism. Only a man who loves in God will be able to refrain from judging and to take everywhere the delight that leads people to God.

⚜

Extend your love to all mankind

Following the example of Christ, who "went about doing good,"[281] charity will be everywhere and always eager to do what good it can. Wherever Providence has placed it, it seeks the good of others, "not considering the things that are his own, but those that are other men's,"[282] but without intruding or imposing itself, for it judges, in all humility, that it is less than anyone.[283]

This concern for others will turn to prayer; in our powerlessness to understand, to advise, and to help, we are like the Apostles and their five barley loaves confronted with the huge crowd of hungry people who are in danger of fainting. We can only take them to the

[281] Acts 10:38.
[282] Phil. 2:4.
[283] Cf. Phil. 2:3.

Master. And, if it pleases Him, by virtue of His blessing, by contact with His grace, the loaves will multiply in the very hands of those who distribute them.[284]

A man who thus knows himself to be the bearer of Christ's love, and is near his brethren, will find in every contact true communion with Christ, for only Christ in us can love in this way.

Furthermore, we must not omit to mention one modern development that brings happiness to the evangelical conscience. Nowadays, when news travels so fast and so far and we know what is happening all over the world, the concept of our neighbor has widened to include the most remote people. It is impossible to remain indifferent to any of them. At the same time, humanity is more conscious of the ties binding it together, even mere economic needs. One of the forms taken by love of our neighbor will be the love of mankind; it is better to prevent disease than to have to treat it; it is better to remedy social injustice than to have to relieve individual distress.

Thus, charity will reach further; Christians must have a lively sense of responsibility and make the most

[284]Cf. Matt. 14:13-21.

use of the possibilities. But here, too, we must keep a careful watch and be on our guard against motives that may slip in without our realizing. The true sign that our love of mankind is really that of Christ is the love we have for each man, even if he angers us or is our enemy. A truly universal love, if it is born of God, will make us nearer to everyone, without exception. If it comes from anything else, it may include hatred and enmity.

It would be sad to confuse the false love of humanity, born of atheism — and which atheism tries to make its most effective instrument — with Christ's way of loving, which should show the reality of His presence in the world. The dimensions that modern methods give to the efficiency and the expression of fraternal charity ought to serve to make the love that Christ has given His people, so that they can continue His work and draw all men to the Father, plainer and stronger than it has ever been.

Chapter Seventeen

Let love for God motivate all that you do

We have already mentioned St. Thomas's doctrine of intention, which, he teaches, gives more value to our prayers in God's sight than even attention, and which involuntary distractions cannot destroy.

God is not concerned with our ideas or our feelings, but with our hearts. It is important to develop this doctrine — one of the most fundamental in the spiritual life — since we are looking for God and are not yet in final possession.

All voluntary and deliberate action involves a reason that inspires it, a choice that determines its direction, and an impulse that moves it toward its goal and provides the strength necessary for the effort. A traveler, wanting to go to a certain place, chooses a route and sets his pace according to his destination and the speed with which he wishes to arrive. Motion toward the goal, force of effort, and choice of means are all inherent in the original design. This is why the Gospel compares it to the single eye that renders the whole body "lightsome";[285] and, again, to the heart, because its secret depths elude human scrutiny, and its vital impulse penetrates everything.

This intention is what concerns God, the only thing that He, who looks in secret, seems to regard; it is of such value that it enables material things, such as eating and drinking, to give "glory to God"; it gives the most insignificant trifles, such as a glass of water given to a poor person, an eternal value; and without it, even the most heroic and the most effective action, such as giving all our goods to feed the poor, becomes valueless. It is easy to understand: God is spirit, and only spirit can reach Him; He is infinite, and with Him nothing but the infinite matters. Only love can reunite us to God; it alone can take us beyond the limits of time and into eternity.

[285]Matt. 6:22.

Let love for God motivate all that you do

❧

Keep your intention fixed on God

This doctrine, then, is of primary importance: it is one of the treasures of the Gospel. The Lord condemned pharisaism, which put the emphasis on works and external forms. He reminded us of the closeness of our relationship with God and the marvelous destiny of those who do His will.

It is a doctrine that lights the life of many who are engaged on insignificant tasks; it teaches them that these are "things of the Father"; it makes them realize that all human and temporal works can become holy and eternal, and it refutes forever the miserable illusion that would banish holiness from humble daily life. And also it reminds those called to high vocations, particularly the highest, which is to spread the Gospel and dispense the divine mysteries, that what God wants more than anything is the intimate and personal intention that binds them to Him. At the same time, it invalidates any standard lower than its own. We cannot call a whim or inclination that is never translated into action an intention. Hell is not paved with good intentions. It is one thing not to be able to do what we want; it is another not to will what we can do. A true will has value in God's sight even before it is realized, and even if it is never realized. On the other hand, a pretended good will that does nothing is, at bottom, a bad will. The parable of the son who said yes and did not work explicitly condemns it.[286]

It would also be wrong to think that a good intention excuses half-hearted actions, or even bad actions (bad, at least, through heedlessness and dislike of effort). Far from being an excuse, such a sham good intention is a condemnation. Neglected work is neglected work, and the negligence is all the graver if it sullies an offering made to God. If anything is to be offered to God, it must be worthy of God. The laws of the Old Testament forbidding the offering in sacrifice of anything blemished or imperfect seem to symbolize this: what is presented to God must be worthy of God.

Moreover, a good resolution that does not result in better or stronger effort is no intention, but an idle whim. Scripture ridicules the lazy, fine talker, always finding some sort of excuse for not making any effort, and, finally, dying of hunger with his field full of thorns.

[286]Matt. 21:28-31.

Let love for God motivate all that you do

It is equally wrong to hide bad intentions under fine-sounding words that have no relation to fact. Wolves in sheep's clothing; impostors who claim knowledge of God in their words, but deny Him by their actions; false prophets to whom God has not spoken: some of these set out to deceive others, but many deceive only themselves.

⚜

Seek God above all things

This brings us back to the original subject: What must our intention be if it is to make us live with God from now on, transcending the necessities of our present state? What sort of intention can match God's tastes?

Scripture indicates the scope of the divine requirements in the words "seeking God" and "pleasing God."

The Biblical notion of "search" is something so sacred, so absolute, that it is used to signify an intention to move toward God. It seems that nothing can be "sought" except God, so Christ is content to say: "He that seeketh, findeth."[287] If we think of the distraught mother whose child has disappeared, of the technician

[287]Matt. 7:8.

prospecting for oil or uranium, of the merchant in the Gospels who sought pearls of great price,[288] or even of the child turning everything upside down to find his favorite ball, we get some idea of "seeking."

Throughout his life, the believer is seeking God, and, in everything, he wishes only to find God; whatever he says or does, he is looking for God. God is his treasure; his heart is with Him, and therefore he cannot leave Him.

Man seeks in this way only because God Himself has sought him and has found him with His grace; man seeks by giving himself to the absoluteness of God, by rising above all created things and using them only to go to God. Seeking implies desire, love, and need; in this case, infinite desire, absolute love, and total need.

The expression "pleasurable to God" — or the more familiar "pleasing to God" — denotes an even greater mystery. How much God must love for His own creature to be able to occupy his mind and be pleasing to Him! What a response such love demands from man — what new ways of existing and acting in the sight of the holiness and love of the Father! To please God is to be what

[288]Cf. Matt. 13:45-46.

He wants and likes. This is the intention that is essential for God's children.

From this, it is plain to see the importance of what spiritual authors call "purity of intention" with the exclusion of all motives of self-interest. It is abundantly clear that the man who seeks God must not be self-seeking; the man who aspires to God must first of all exclude everything that separates him from Him and displeases Him. Equally obviously in their solitude, their vigils, and their toils and prayers, the fathers of the desert aimed at only one thing: purity of heart.

The light thrown by modern psychology on the unconscious mind, and the whole dark world that threatens resolutions we think inviolate, confirms this doctrine and behooves us to be constantly alert if we are not to be surprised and deceive ourselves into substituting something less for true charity.

But if we think of purity of intention as a negative thing, we make a great mistake. If we intend to please the Father, we must share in His tastes, let ourselves be carried into the depths where God loves Himself, and grow to the measure of this love. It is not enough for a Christian to avoid what is displeasing to God; he must gladly accept whatever pleases Him, not recoiling from the daunting climb. "Father, I will that where I am, they also whom Thou hast given me may be with me."[289] Let us read these words again and again as an infinitely wonderful promise; the transformation that carries us above ourselves is set in motion by this promise. The child of God must come to have God's own intentions; the purity of intention that seems at first a purely personal effort ends in the closest communion with God teaching us to think and act as He does.

When the wise man counseled his disciples to be to God as the "apple of His eye"[290] and so to find the right way of looking at everything, he was teaching them this great lesson; that one must forget himself in order to come face-to-face with God. "But we have the mind of Christ."[291]

⚜

Judge the purity of your intention by your actions

How can we realize such an ideal? It is no use merely to say that it is a gift of grace and we can only ask for it

[289]John 17:24.
[290]Ps. 16:8 (RSV = Ps. 17:8).
[291]1 Cor. 2:16.

and wait for it; we need to be constantly on the watch for any egotistical self-seeking, to be always alert and concerned to "seek to please God."

It may be good to deal with a few special points. Christ spoke of this intention and thus indicated the importance of the faith that sets us in God's horizon, perspective, and light. This is why anything that develops faith, keeps it alive, or broadens or illumines it is extremely important.

And here spiritual reading comes into its own. Without it, our faith could easily deteriorate into little more than a formula, and we would live and react according to human standards instead of God's.

We must reorientate ourselves time and again by the great perspectives opened to us by Christ's prayer after the Last Supper and also by, for instance, the letters to the Ephesians and to the Colossians. An intention that clings mainly to self, to its own conscience and inclinations, quickly lapses; if it is to have strength, breadth, and beauty, it must cling to God and to His intentions. Prayer must become more and more centered in God, placing and replacing itself where it can contemplate the love with which God loves us, so that Christ may live within us.

A true intention is also necessary to combat the dangers of routine and tepidity. It is certainly clear, from what has been said, that intention is at the heart of action and that it lives through the existence of action. A traveler does not need to tell himself at every step that he is going to a particular place; it is merely necessary for him to continue walking. Similarly, in spiritual realities, the best sign of the truth and efficacy of the intention is the action it promotes: a tree is recognized by its fruits.

For the love of Christ, I will treat every unknown person as my brother in God; the genuineness of this intention will be proved, not by my remembering it, but by the devotion, understanding, and consideration that I show toward any and every person who asks me to do him a service. We must never lose sight of it; nor may we ask how long it will last, since it lasts as long as it urges the conscience and spurs it on, as long as it enlightens and inspires our life.

Yet, like all man's spirituality, intention will weaken if it is not nourished. The youthful vigor of a soul is shown by the working in it of its reasons for action. Therefore, we must return often, indeed continuously, with each new action to the love that must be the inspiration and the measure of all else: "God has loved me so greatly. He wishes to have me as a workman helping to build His kingdom. What kind of day ought this to be? What kind of hour? What kind of action?"

Part Three

❧

*Achieving life
with God*

Chapter Eighteen

ൟ

Grow closer to God
through spiritual reading

I am now going to stress, perhaps unduly, one of the most effective stimulants of life with God — namely, spiritual reading. It is particularly important for Christians living in the world who have little time and must therefore keep a strict watch on the quality of their efforts. Life in the world is treacherous, and it is easy to slip away from the gospel if we do not strive energetically to prevent it.

Christ asked His people, sent to the world and for the world, for holiness in truth, and if, as He adds, this truth is God's word, we must not forget that this word is repeated to us by the whole Church through the voice of her children, from the greatest to the smallest.

It is impossible to have a part in God's friendship unless we make use of the infinite treasure of His wisdom. He alone is the Master, but His teaching is repeated to us by His disciples, both in their writings and in their spoken words. We must have deep, personal convictions to be able to live life fully and deal easily and vigorously with unforeseen circumstances; in the world, the Christian is like a lamb among wolves, and he must be both simple and prudent.[292]

The principles by which human thought tries to model itself on God's thought are the props that support life. They are the skeleton, while the external, negative rules remind us of the shells that protect soft creatures, but restrict their movements. Such wisdom can be learned only gradually by keeping company with the wise men whose books we wear out because we cannot sit at their feet.[293] In this way, we obtain a true knowledge that is not an accumulation of sterile ideas, but an inward strength increasingly united and receptive.

Yet it would be foolish to pretend that spiritual reading is without its dangers, or that it always achieves so

[292]Cf. Matt. 10:16.
[293]Cf. Ecclus. 6:36 (RSV = Sir. 6:36).

high an end. Human nature can grasp an idea or a formula more quickly than it can understand it or put it into practice; sometimes knowing something theoretically makes us forget how much we really lack it. It is in this sense particularly that all men are liars. One man says things he does not know; another says things that he does not do.

This evil is increased today by the diffuseness of current ideas, which belong to all and to nobody, since everyone repeats them, and no one admits responsibility for them. Beautiful ideas can remain in the consciousness like foreign bodies, not making life better and sometimes being betrayed or disfigured by life. Reading enriches us with other people's ideas, but can make parrots of us, not in the sense that we repeat the ideas of others — for, in fact, is there anything that we know which we do not derive in one way or another from the Christian community? — but because we repeat things that we do not understand, that we do not ourselves know, that do not bring new life to our spirit. Our ideas remain things we have instead of things that make us live better and grow closer to truth. Here more than elsewhere, we have to fear the danger of half-truths and lies that would keep us from the truth. How could we then be with God? For "His communication is with the simple,"[294] with those in whom there is neither duplicity nor lying. What, then, are we to do?

Read so as to grow closer to Christ

The less time we have, the more important is our choice of books. It would be tragic if fashion or curiosity crept in where our object is to come closer to God and to be in tune with His thought so as to enter into intimacy and to fulfill His purposes better.

Moreover, it is not a question of reading with the eyes only, or retaining in the memory, but of understanding, of taking each thought and assimilating it by interpreting it, trying to see its meaning and significance, finding out its relation to some part of God's word, and looking to see how it may be applied; by observing which of our ideas it contradicts and which it upholds, what it demands of our life, what it can give to the world, and how it ought best be handed on to those whom it might save. To have read a few pages of a book, or even the whole of it, is not particularly useful, but to

[294]Prov. 3:32.

have made progress, however small, in the knowledge of God, of His love and His purposes, is an infinite treasure.

Every time we become better disciples of Christ, the Father is glorified. This is another way of saying that in all our reading, we must seek to learn from Christ, tracing His thoughts in those of the author. As soon as we have assimilated an idea, it must be put back into its place in the divine light. We must know ourselves "taught of God,"[295] and if an idea is not to become an empty formula, we must first seek its value in relation to Christ, then pray about it, speak to Him of it, and learn its application, its demands, and its potentialities, so that, believing more truly and having better surrendered our minds to truth, our ties with Him will become more personal and more living.

Even if this way of reading takes longer, it must not for that reason be abandoned. How can time be better used than by growing in "friendship with God"? But it is really less a matter of time than a question of soul and of interior attitude. The main thing is to be a "disciple," to be completely open to the Master's thoughts, to be in

[295] John 6:45.

direct relationship with His teaching, or rather, with His personality; His teachings are the most personal confidences, for they make us His friends in the sense in which the Master of all truth speaks of friendship.

Such thinking, progressively developed, will enlighten all our reading, our experiences, and the sermons we hear; it will make the life of our mind more attentive, more objective, and more genuine, because it is established in light. Spiritual reading that does not result in self-forgetfulness and true enlightenment is certainly not fulfilling its function and is a "pious practice," not a study of God's word.

Chapter Nineteen

⚜

Avoid falling into routine
in your spiritual life

A friendship that is free and spontaneous nevertheless needs rites and forms of expression; witness the fox's lessons to the Little Prince.[296] What is true in the human order is even truer when God draws man to his friendship. These rites, on God's side, are the sacraments. On the Church's part, they are the liturgical cycle. On the part of the individual, they are the duties that dictate the rhythm of spiritual life.

It is foolish to leave everything to the whim of the moment under the pretext of spontaneity. To do this is to take no precaution whatever against the weak and

[296] Antoine de St. Exupéry, *The Little Prince*.

changeable nature of man; we would run the danger of forgetting all guidance as to the best paths, all the desires we have experienced, and all the conclusions we have reached as to what our spiritual life needs to keep its impetus and vigor. The man of the parable who sits down to work out the cost of building his tower has to know where his supplies will come from, and what the building conditions are.[297] We can apply this parable to every stage of our progress, and it will remind us that the Christian life is based, not on any human code, but on the absolute to which the divine friendship summons it.

❧

Determine your spiritual needs

For many people, the temporal rhythm of their supernatural lives is fixed by the spiritual family to which they belong, by their religious rule, or by the directives given to them by various authorities. Through them, the members share in the wisdom of their founders; they cannot live their rule well unless they become united with the founders' intentions. For others, there are the general laws of the Church, as in the case of priests. But

[297]Cf. Luke 14:28-30.

in each case, there will be the personal way the individual builds his life within the framework. Finally, some will discover the rule that is to guide them in their progress by their own prudence.

Often, the immediate necessities are confined to work, travel, and other human affairs, but necessity, which Pascal called one of the masters given by God, can provide the means for anyone who is willing to submit to it. It is necessary, on the one hand, to decide what nourishment our spiritual life normally needs. First, of course, are the sacraments that unite us to Christ. Then comes the need for personal renewals, so that the God-centered life can enter explicitly into communion with God; and the frequency, rhythm, and quality of these should tend to make life an act of charity. Equally necessary are the prayers made or proposed by the Church to lift up our own prayer and make it part of the prayer of the Church, principally by the Liturgy and then by the secondary forms she offers.

On the other hand, faith needs to be enlightened and roused by a living contact with God's word, and by the Church's teaching. It also needs to be aware of its place in the world, of the problems that confront it, and the solutions it offers. Now, more than ever, because of the size and new forms of the problems, a Christian cannot lead a spiritual life without permanent contact with the life of the Church and the researches and thought of his brethren. These are the essential materials for building a life in communion with God.

Having made this inventory of our needs, we must remember that in a life crammed with unexpected interruptions, it is much less a timetable we need than a scale of values. We must not forget also that in modern life, where work and daily occupations encroach on the nighttime, and a daily rhythm is often impossible, we can substitute a weekly, monthly, or even yearly pattern.

Apply effort and concentration to all that you do for God

Yet this is not the important thing. As in all that concerns life with God, what matters is within, is the quality; it is less important what we do than how we do it. If we are enlightened by the Spirit, we shall find great riches in any book; if we are not, we shall miss the depths of a spiritual masterpiece and draw nothing from it of the least use for life; ready-made prayers can be affectation and routine for one person, depth and life for another.

To preserve this inward quality and to avoid the materialism that threatens spiritual life in the world, two dispositions seem of primary importance. First, never do anything for the purpose of getting it over with, or getting rid of it, as if it were a debt. Nothing we do can seem to us great, or sufficient to satisfy God. Whatever we do, we know that God deserves infinitely more, and we are far below the standard of His love; even our own love is not content with it and wants to do more. At prayer, we want to give ourselves and say the eternal yes that responds to God's presence; when reading, we want to communicate with God's wisdom.

It is always necessary to put the maximum effort and concentration into what we do for God; to remember why, or, better, for whom, we do it. Routine is a threat to spiritual life; there is always the risk of making some particular gesture because we have always done it, and because the promise to do it was given to ourselves and not to God.

To escape routine, it is necessary to remember the inward value of a given exercise. Saying the Rosary is meant to bring us into communion with the soul of our

Lady and Him who is its life; a particular reading answers a certain need. From time to time, we ought to question ourselves about what we are doing, and the way we are doing it, and also to fight the staleness of custom by some change, by a better-adapted program, and so on.

Here, as in all else, the only question put to a Christian's love is, in the end, simply what is Christ's point of view. The disciple thinks only of giving; he will judge by reference, not to himself, but to God; he will be strict and at the same time free, knowing how to continue and how to change, how to cling and to renounce so that the divine life that is in him among the anxieties and limitations of time may still fulfill the eternal intention.

Chapter Twenty

⚜

Abide in God
through the Eucharist

To fulfill His wish to have us with Him, Christ instituted the Eucharist even before showing us His glory. He who is "in the bosom of the Father" receives "in His bosom" the disciple whom he loves.[298] The Gospel uses the same phrase as if to make us reflect on this intimacy with Christ which leads us to His Father. We shall not attempt to study here the whole of the eucharistic mystery, but only insofar as it is as an initiation into or a fulfillment of the life with God.

The choice of bread expresses better than any words the Lord's intention of giving Himself to us, placing

[298]Cf. John 1:18, 13:23.

Himself at our service, making us live His life. To make us understand how profound is the intimacy He wishes to give us, Christ compares it with that which unites Him to the Father; there can be no closer intimacy, no more loving dependence, no life more generously shared: "He that eateth my flesh and drinketh my blood abideth in me, and I in him. As the living Father hath sent me and I live by the Father, so he that eateth me, the same also shall live by me."[299] The transformation will extend even to the body, which one day will rise again.

We are dealing here with a spiritual reality and relationship that is not dependent on the senses, or even wholly on sacramental Communion — that is, communion through a sign. The Church, in the Council of Trent, affirmed the value of the "spiritual" communion, which feeds on the Eucharist by faith, desire, and rejection of self, independent of external circumstances.

It is also certain that the Lord, the best judge of human conditions, gave Himself to us under the appearance of bread to make us realize the daily and progressive character of our transformation in Him. There is no question of a sudden spectacular result, for that is

---

[299] John 6:57-58 (RSV = John 6:56-57).

not God's way; it is an infinitely subtle invasion by the truest of loves.

Yet we have to ask ourselves how we can remain so self-centered, so hard, and so indifferent after so many Communions? How can we be daily in touch with fire without burning? Obviously we lack some essential.

One such essential is that we must share by faith in the mind of God. It is not enough to affirm the Real Presence of Christ, Body, Blood, Soul, and Godhead; we must also accept the mystery and surrender to its purposes, if we are to understand its love. This is the "fullness of faith" that St. Paul commended. Lack of awareness in faith might well obstruct the divine action.

⚜

Offer yourself to God in the Mass

A second essential is to enter fully into the eucharistic mystery. There is a danger here of dividing what is one; multiplicity of devotions weakens the vitality of faith. If we separate the Eucharist from God's plan as a whole, or Mass and Communion from the rest of our life, some of its force is lost. It ought to be impossible for us to pray without remembering that God made us: "He that spared not even His own Son, but delivered Him up for us all, how has He not also, with Him, given us all things?"[300] It ought to be impossible for us to open the Gospel without remembering our Lord's gift of Himself and His infinitely faithful friendship. Then everything would appear in its true light. We should also understand to what degree the Lord's love is really personal: "He has loved me and has delivered Himself for me."[301] Similarly, every Communion ought to remind us of the life and death of the Lord. The Lord we receive is the very same who suffered for us, died for us, and rose again. One day we shall meet Him and live with Him eternally. In this light, the whole of our inward life is changed and quickened by our Communion.

Finally, to fulfill the divine intention, it is of first importance for us to share fully in the Mass. St. Ignatius of Antioch,[302] in one of his letters, compares Christ to a hoist. He has to lift us out of ourselves to join us to Him, to make us enter into His intentions and cooperate in His work. If we are to identify ourselves with the Mass,

---

[300] Rom. 8:32.

[301] Gal. 2:20.

[302] St. Ignatius of Antioch (d. c. 107), disciple of John the Evangelist, bishop, and martyr.

we must share, not only the priest's prayers, but his mind.

On this subject, Pope Pius XII said, "In order that the oblation, by which in this Sacrifice they offer to the heavenly Father the divine Victim, may obtain its full effect, Christians themselves must add something: they must immolate themselves as victims. Such an immolation is not restricted only to the liturgical sacrifice. Because we are built upon Christ as a living rock, the Prince of Apostles desires that we may, as a holy priesthood, offer victims spiritually agreeable to God through Jesus Christ. And the apostle Paul, speaking for all time, exhorts the faithful in these terms: 'I conjure you, then, my brethren, that you offer your bodies as a living, holy victim, agreeable to God; this is the spiritual worship that you owe to Him.'

"But when the faithful share in the liturgical action with so much piety and attention that one can say of them that their 'faith and devotion are known,' then it is impossible that the faith of each one should not act with more ardor through charity, that their piety should not become strengthened and more burning, that they should not consecrate themselves, each and all, to procure God's glory and, in their fervent desire to make themselves strictly like to Jesus Christ, who suffered most cruel pains, it is impossible that they should not offer themselves with and through the Supreme Priest, as a spiritual host."[303]

Then there is thanksgiving, the value of which has been confirmed by modern theologians; certainly, the sacrifice is in itself a thanksgiving, but Christ as Priest wishes to offer us with Him so that the Father will accept us as victims of praise. His sacrifice is made complete in us in the sense that He offers us with Him and in Him; and, in the words of the Pope Pius XII, "He likes to hear our prayers, to speak to us with an open heart, and to offer us a refuge in His heart." This thanksgiving makes us "take on the likeness of Christ and through Him orientate ourselves toward the heavenly Father."[304] In any case, thanksgiving must not stop at a given moment; it ought to last as long as life. If we reduce thanksgiving to an exercise, when we owe our whole life to Him who gave Himself to us, we are in danger of isolation and consequent disintegration. This brings us to the third point.

[303] *Mediator Dei*.
[304] Ibid.

Abide in God through the Eucharist

❧

Seek union with your neighbor

Jesus Christ desires that our union with Him should unite us also with all the other members of His Body, that it should be both the sign and the cause of the brotherly unity that He has most at heart. Above all, at the altar it is necessary to remember any quarrel we may have, for no offering can be presented until we are reconciled. Sharing the Bread unites all the members together in one body. So that if Communion is to unite us to Christ, as He is united to the Father, we must let it join us one to the other, and must learn from Him to give ourselves to our brethren as He has given Himself to us.[305] St. Augustine expressed it by explaining to his followers that the fact of having been invited to the Prince's table laid on them an obligation to respond to His gift by giving themselves to their brethren.

This communion in the love with which Christ loves men clearly brings us back to our problem. Insofar as we allow Christ to transform us by His Eucharist, we shall share in the union of life that binds us to Him and makes us live by Him, as He lives by the Father.

[305]Cf. 1 John 3:16.

The Eucharist exemplifies the whole plan of the great love of God, who wishes to unite us to Him, but it does so in a veiled way: the supreme self-abasement of God throws light on our own condition; it shows the contrast between the truth of His love, which gives all, and the weakness of man's temporal state, which hides all and makes all frail: "Behold what manner of charity the Father hath bestowed upon us, that we should be called and be the sons of God. Therefore the world knoweth not us, because it knew not Him. Dearly beloved, we are now the sons of God; and it hath not yet appeared what we shall be. We know that when He shall appear we shall be like to Him, because we shall see Him as He is."[306]

The Eucharist affirms this love in a way fitting to our state as travelers; it tells us again the meaning of our life, our vocation as children of God in Christ to serve, near Him, the apprenticeship for life with the Father; thus we shall best respond to the love that wants to take us with Him. "I will come again and take you to myself."[307]

[306] 1 John 3:1-2.
[307] John 14:3.

Fr. Joseph-Marie Perrin, O.P.

Although he was blind from the age of ten, Joseph-Marie Perrin was able to enter the Dominican Order and lead a very active apostolic life, during which his handicap sometimes brought him unexpected meetings and friendships. In 1937, he founded Caritas Christi, a secular institute. This international foundation required him to do a great deal of traveling; he met the challenge with aplomb in spite of his handicap.

During World War II, Fr. Perrin was active in the French resistance to the tyranny and inhumanity of the Nazis. He took particular risks by helping Jews escape from France. For this courageous work, he was imprisoned by the Gestapo in 1943. In 2000, he was awarded the prize of Righteous Gentile, or Just among the Nations, by the State of Israel and the Yad Vachem Institute for the south of France. This prize was a gesture of recognition for Fr. Perrin's heroic efforts to save Jews during World War II, even at the risk of his own life.

Although in his nineties, Fr. Perrin spoke movingly at this event, reminding those present that, although he was the one being honored, they are all brothers who acted with courage at that time: those who lived and those who died.

Also during World War II, Fr. Perrin became close friends with Simone Weil, the famous French philosopher and religious seeker. Weil's classic book *Waiting for God* emerged from discussions and correspondence she had with Fr. Perrin. Although she ultimately rejected his offer to baptize her into the Catholic Faith, Weil did come to see — with Fr. Perrin's help — the truth of Christianity.

Fr. Perrin is the author of about thirty books, mostly devoted to the life of laypeople in the world.

can help Sophia Institute Press® to provide the public with editions of works containing the enduring wisdom of the ages. Please send your tax-deductible contribution to the address below. We also welcome your questions, comments, and suggestions.

For your free catalog, call:
Toll-free: 1-800-888-9344

or write:
Sophia Institute Press®
Box 5284, Manchester, NH 03108

or visit our website:
www.sophiainstitute.com

Sophia Institute™ is a tax-exempt institution
as defined by the Internal Revenue Code,
Section 501(c)(3). Tax I.D. 22-2548708.